Tony Carter

Customer Advisory Boards
A Strategic Tool
for Customer Relationship Building

Pre-publication
REVIEWS,
COMMENTARIES,
EVALUATIONS . . .

"It has become fashionable for large and small companies alike to incorporate customer advisory boards (CABs) into their organizations. The stated purpose of these boards is to ensure that the voice of the customer is reflected in the decisions and actions of the organizations. While this is an admirable objective, it is our experience that too often these boards fail to achieve their goal. Tony Carter has provided a thorough and practical guide toward the use of CABs.

Particularly useful are Carter's thought-provoking questions, which should cause senior manager to pause before running headlong into the selection of a CAB. In addition, the author's use of case studies enables the reader to better understand the causes of failure and the requirements of success for CABs. I highly recommend this book to those who are contemplating building a CAB and to those who may already have a CAB in their company but are looking for a way to improve its impact on their organization's success."

Mel Ingold, MS
Adjunct Professor,
Columbia University Executive Programs;
Director, Impact Planning Group

More pre-publication
REVIEWS, COMMENTARIES, EVALUATIONS . . .

"**S**trategy is an 'outside in' process that requires in part a superior understanding of the customer if a business is going to win. Tony Carter's *Customer Advisory Boards: A Strategic Tool for Customer Relationship Building* has provided the reader with a tool to understand the customer. Research supports the importance of using this tool if a company wants to gain competitive advantage—a customer advisory board (CAB), 'provides a continuing dialogue with current and potential customers instead of the static information of market research.'

In addition to the why, what, and how of CABs, Carter makes the direct link of emotional intelligence (EI) of the executive leader in the building of customer alliances. This chapter alone is worth the cost of the book. But if that doesn't convince you, Carter has also linked his work to that of many successful companies and given particular attention to global businesses. All in all, a solid piece of scholarship and writing."

William M. Klepper, PhD
Academic Director, Executive Education,
Columbia Graduate School of Business

"**I**n this latest book, *Customer Advisory Boards,* Tony Carter has again focused attention on another important aspect of business practice. The objective of marketing is to first discover and then fulfill the demands of customers. This may be achieved by building strong customer relationships through the establishment of CABs. By obtaining specific information from existing and potential customers, a firm may supply a market with those goods and services that are wanted and needed. This strategic tool is ultimately based on the ability to listen. A number of case studies are presented including global applications. I strongly recommend that this book be read by executives and managers. It is original and dynamic work."

Walter F. Rohrs, PhD
Professor Emeritus,
Wagner College

BEST
BUSINESS
BOOKS

Best Business Books®
An Imprint of The Haworth Press, Inc.
New York • London • Oxford

Customer Advisory Boards
A Strategic Tool
for Customer Relationship Building

BEST BUSINESS BOOKS
Robert E. Stevens, PhD
David L. Loudon, PhD
Editors in Chief

Strategic Planning for Collegiate Athletics by Deborah A. Yow,
R. Henry Migliore, William W. Bowden, Robert E. Stevens,
and David L. Loudon

*Church Wake-Up Call: A Ministries Management Approach That
Is Purpose-Oriented and Inter-Generational in Outreach*
by William Benke and Le Etta N. Benke

Organizational Behavior by O. Jeff Harris and Sandra J. Hartman

Marketing Research: Text and Cases by Bruce Wrenn, Robert Stevens,
and David Loudon

Doing Business in Mexico: A Practical Guide by Gus Gordon
and Thurmon Williams

Employee Assistance Programs in Mananged Care by Norman Winegar

*Marketing Your Business: A Guide to Developing a Strategic Marketing
Plan* by Ronald A. Nykiel

*Customer Advisory Boards: A Strategic Tool for Customer Relationship
Building* by Tony Carter

Fundamentals of Business Marketing Research by David A. Reid
and Richard E. Plank

Marketing Management: Text and Cases by David L. Loudon,
Robert E. Stevens, and Bruce Wrenn

Selling in the New World of Business by Bob Kimball
and Jerold "Buck" Hall

Customer Advisory Boards
A Strategic Tool
for Customer Relationship Building

Tony Carter

Best Business Books®
An Imprint of The Haworth Press, Inc.
New York • London • Oxford

Published by

Best Business Books®, an imprint of The Haworth Press, Inc., 10 Alice Street, Binghamton, NY 13904-1580.

Chapter 3 is a revised and expanded version of Chapter 4, "Customer Focus," in Tony Carter, *The Aftermath of Reengineering: Downsizing and Corporate Performance* (Binghamton, NY: The Haworth Press, 1999).

Cover design by Marylouise E. Doyle.

Library of Congress Cataloging-in-Publication Data

Carter, Tony, 1955-
    Customer advisory boards : a strategic tool for customer relationship building / Tony Carter.
      p. cm.
    Includes bibliographical references and index.
    ISBN 0-7890-1557-9 (case : alk. paper) — ISBN 0-7890-1558-7 (soft : alk. paper)
    1. Customer advisory boards. 2. Customer services—Management. 3. Customer relations—Management. 4. Relationship marketing. I. Title.

HF5415.523.C37 2003
658.8'12—dc22
                                         2003014670

The inspiration for this book
is my soul mate, Tia, and our love
and Calvin and Walter,
whom I love deeply as sons, men, and teammates.

ABOUT THE AUTHOR

Tony Carter, JD, MBA, is Professor at the Christos M. Cotsakos College of Business, William Paterson University in The Russ Berrie Institute for Professional Sales in Wayne, New Jersey. In addition, he is Adjunct Professor of Marketing at the Graduate School of Business of Columbia University, where he teaches in the MBA program and has taught in the Executive MBA program. At Columbia University, Dr. Carter is also Associate Faculty Director of the Executive Management Programs for Sales Management and Key Account Management. In 1994-1995, he was the General Mills visiting professor at the Columbia University Graduate School of Business.

The author of the books *Contemporary Sales Force Management, The Aftermath of Reengineering,* and the present volume (The Haworth Press, Inc.), Dr. Carter has written articles that have been published in the *Harvard Business Review,* the *Columbia Journal of World Business, Business Week,* the *Journal of Professional Services Marketing,* the *Journal of Global Competitiveness, Sales and Marketing Management, Management Magazine, Selling Power,* the *Journal of Economic Literatures,* the *Journal of Personal Selling and Sales Management,* and the *Journal of Employment.* He is the Editor-in-Chief of the *Journal of Hospital Marketing and Public Relations.*

Dr. Carter has worked as a manager for several corporations and has been a guest lecturer at universities overseas, such as the Caucasus School of Business in Tbilisi, Georgia. His case studies and research on marketing, sales, and management have been adopted and used by various universities and organizations around the world. Dr. Carter has conducted research in the European Union in Belgium, The People's Republic of China, and Poland. Still an active consultant, he works on management, sales, and marketing issues for a variety of companies worldwide. Dr. Carter is the recipient of The Wall Street Journal Award and other awards for his publications, and is an inductee of Delta Mu Delta, The National Honor Society in Business Administration.

CONTENTS

SECTION II: BUILDING CUSTOMER ADVISORY BOARDS

SECTION III: STRATEGIC USES AND EFFECTIVE MANAGEMENT

Foreword

In today's extremely competitive, high-cost environment, Tony Carter has discovered a creative and unique answer to the major question of every CEO: "How can we hold onto customers after we finally get them on the books and using our products?" The customer advisory board (CAB) can be the solution for any organization, whether a major industrial corporation, a religious institution, or even a local 7-Eleven. Your CAB can help in answering your challenging questions concerning why we do things a certain way and why we should think of trying a new approach. This book is guaranteed to stoke your creative fires!

Donald W. Spiro, Chairman,
Oppenheimer Management Corporation

Preface and Acknowledgments

In business, as with personal life, strong meaningful relationships are the key to better understanding and satisfaction. The catch is recognizing that understanding is everything because it leads to deeper insights about other people and their needs, thus enabling corporations to give them what they need. Today, people are quite unique and distinct about their needs, and the most effective suppliers do not just consider themselves helpers' pawns who respond to any whims that their clients convey. Instead, they are secure in the understanding that the most effective sellers today know that the strongest competitive advantage comes by giving customers exactly what they want, which is extremely demanding for any organization in business today. That a customer can say, "That is what I need if you want my business; otherwise I'll go somewhere else," seems to empower the customer. However, it really does not; it just means that customers can redefine value and where they will spend their money. The control that drives deals and business transactions will still be with the sellers, if they are discerning and creative enough to capitalize on these opportunities. The challenge for sales is how to capture and regularly satisfy an always changing, demanding, and sophisticated buyer with high expectations.

Customer advisory boards (CABs) are an extraordinary and successful tool that gives organizations the opportunity, in a nonthreatening setting, to get closer to their clients. The chance for decision makers to learn what it takes for a seller to be the kind of firm a customer will buy from is a very compelling, dynamic encounter.

I wrote this book to show the importance of relationships in business and how CABs can be used as a competitive tool. I have included results from surveys with several hundred Fortune 500 and midsized firms to illustrate how these companies and their customers are responding to issues through the use of CABs. These boards have many ancillary benefits such as relationship building, customer and industry information, improved communication, market research, research and development, and trust.

I would like to acknowledge some important people in my life who have shown me the importance of relationship building: my sons, Calvin and Walter; my wife, Tia; my parents; Walter Palin; as well as Mike, Kerstein, Kim, Kirk, and Mikey. My professional family of Dr. Walter Rohrs of Wagner College; Dr. Noel Capon of Columbia University; Dr. Don Spiro of Oppenheimer Management Corporation; George King, CEO of 20/20 Advisory Partners; and Ambassador Ulric Haynes always serve as inspirations by their examples, hard work, and encouragement. The editorial staff of The Haworth Press have been very helpful on this book project; Bill Palmer and Amy Rentner, in particular, have been great to work with, as always. A special thanks to Arlene Wilk, whose help was greatly appreciated.

SECTION I:
CUSTOMER RELATIONSHIP BUILDING

Chapter 1

Introduction:
A Way to Reach Customers

A dynamic, practical sales tool that can greatly enhance the customer development and retention process and give firms a distinct competitive advantage is the customer advisory board (CAB). A board can help a sales force broaden its decision-making expertise and generate more business. Sales involves more than an upbeat personality and hard work. It involves product or service knowledge, a proficiency in selling, an awareness of market conditions, and adding value to what the customer is doing. Industries and markets that are changing rapidly, due to globalization and advancing technology, pose a more complex business environment today. Thus, some firms have a customer advisory board, or its equivalent, to act as an advisory and management auxiliary resource in the face of these conditions.[1] (For specific activities of CABs see Figure 1.1.)

FIGURE 1.1. Role of CABs in the Marketplace

Customer retention is more complex than ever before and there has been a dramatic change in how selling takes place. Customer relationship building is a driving force in the selling process. To assess what entails an effective sales effort, companies must first identify why their customers chose them. It is essential to have a clear understanding of what customers want and concentrate on providing it. In a study conducted by Learning International, 29 percent of 210 corporate customers with vendors in the technology, financial services, and pharmaceutical industries reported that business expertise and image ranked highest among various attributes that lead to satisfaction levels with a supplier.[2]

Instead of selecting what a company has to offer, today's customer tells the company what he or she wants; it is then up to the company to figure out how to supply it. These customers present some important questions that must be answered:

How can a product or service be differentiated when rising quality is forcing industries toward the same standard?
How do you distinguish what customers are saying and what they really mean?
Where can you find your best customers?
What service levels please customers most?
How do you hold on to current customers?

Thus, identifying relevant customer information is the essence of having the competitive advantage. A CAB can provide this edge and strengthen a company's presence in the marketplace.

AN OVERVIEW OF THE CAB

A board is far more effective than advisers because board members are empowered to offer advice that can affect the company.[3] Allowing outsiders to look inside the workings of your company can lead to a feeling of vulnerability, and in fact only 5 percent of closely held companies actually do allow their boards to be dominated by outsiders.[4] CABs, which essentially target actual prospective customers as members, are a cost-effective way to find out directly from the marketplace how to become a firm with which customers would initiate or continue to do business. Their feedback also provides a fresh perspective from which to approach business opportunities. (For an overview of the dynamics faced by CABs in relationship building, see Figure 1.2.)

The advisory board is more informal than the board of directors and counsels without the voting power and legal liability to protect shareholder interest. To be manageable a board should have five to ten members or as many as twelve to fifteen members who are prominent in the business community. Companies can even use a revolving board that changes membership every one to two years to broaden the pool of participants.

The length of tenure for board members can be short or long term depending on the needs and circumstances of the company and the board members. For example, a membership period of one to two years allows for more frequent influx of new members and the perspectives that they bring through their participation. Longer-term memberships provide a more stable, familiar board presence.

The board can meet quarterly or more frequently, as circumstances dictate. In the event of a crisis or emergency situation, the board may

FIGURE 1.2. Dynamics of Today's Challenges for Effective Customer Development and Dealings

actually provide a company with a fuller range of perspectives to help overcome the dilemma. At a minimum, boards should meet at least twice a year to be of some strategic utility, which means they need not be a totally time-consuming endeavor to provide some clear benefit.[5]

The CAB can be comprised of CEOs and presidents or the functional executives who decide where they will direct their business. Members could be selected for their particular expertise. For example, a strategic planner with a good long-range perspective or a technical expert who understands a product's or service's features might be a good choice.[6] Other favored board candidates are women and minorities, who can reflect a diversity of views and insights that can be of great benefit to a firm. Members could also be selected for their demographic segment, geographical location, revenue potential, reputation, and prestige in the marketplace.

Board membership can serve as a perk for current customers and reward them for their loyalty or reach prospective customers who do not currently use a company. Customers want to believe that companies care, and the formation of a CAB alone can show this and help to develop a rapport. Board membership also makes it possible for the various professionals on the board to network with one another. Membership can also be a stamp of success for candidates who accept companies' invitations since the criteria for selection are their prominence and knowledge. Thus, a unique feature of CABs is that the members expect their advice to be taken seriously.

In 1998, companies spent $3.5 billion with the fifty biggest research firms to learn about their customers. Market research can be extremely valuable but is expensive and can be done fraudulently. Companies can wield the information that comes out of board meetings as one source of market research, and as a way to study the psychology of buyer behavior in order to enhance sales.[7] In many cases, a CAB can be operated without any fees. The rationale for this, besides being cost-effective, is to avoid any appearance of impropriety, such as an attempt to "buy business," relying instead on the members' expertise in solely an advisory capacity.

An effective board encourages the participation of the sales force and management personnel. Their suggestions help target desired board members and frame the relevant issues to be discussed when the board meets. In addition, their involvement with the board places them in the position to build relationships. Sales management should also be involved with the board so as to signal a serious commitment on the part of the corporation to provide high-level feedback that can impact company policy.

A critical role for the board is helping to identify and resolve strategy and performance issues. This means that board members must have a solid understanding of both industry and individual functions as well as knowing what creates value in the business. The board members should be routinely informed about relevant company, industry, and economic events. They should receive the appropriate press clippings, subscriptions to selected industry journals, and any other relevant information that will keep them informed. Board members should know the concerns and thoughts of the people working in the company and what the competition is doing.

To maximize the effectiveness of the advisory board a company should raise certain questions early in the board's formation and operation to allow for necessary adjustments later on:

1. Do you want board members who act as thought partners concerning the major issues facing the business?
2. Can you count on the board to give you fully informed and objective opinions?
3. Is the company getting full value from the board?
4. Is the board's perception of your performance in tune with your own?
5. If not, are you concerned about the ramifications of that discrepancy should the company's performance take a turn for the worse?

Many firms have a CAB or its equivalent. Fortune 500 firms such as IBM, Merck & Co., and The Equitable have found them to be extremely helpful in their customer relationship–building process.

THE CUSTOMER RELATIONSHIP–BUILDING PROCESS

This involves a company's commitment to build rapport with customers and to provide a valuable service through that relationship. This process requires consulting customers for preferences, gaining familiarity and knowledge of customers, and conducting business in a customized fashion. The process provides companies with the opportunity to build customer satisfaction with each customer contact. It is an important process to set in motion.

Customers today are more demanding, sophisticated, and educated, and they are quite comfortable speaking to companies as equals. They have more customized expectations and want to be treated as individuals. They know their business best, so the opportunity to listen to them through the dialogue generated by having an advisory board will help uncover how best to meet their needs.

The customer relationship–building process is necessary because two-thirds of all revenue comes from current customers, and cultivating new customers costs about four to five times more than maintaining existing customers. Also, 91 percent of unhappy customers will never buy again from a company that dissatisfied them, and they will communicate their displeasure to other people. These dissatisfied customers may not even convey their displeasure to the company, but simply stop doing business with that company, leaving the company unaware that there is a problem. Customers become dissatisfied with a company for various reasons that are generally focused on product or service quality, price, lack of attentiveness, complacency, poor location, no customer complaint system, or a weak public image.

Considering that about one-third of all dissatisfied customers leave because they felt unappreciated and some dissatisfied customers never complain to the company, monitoring customer satisfaction becomes a primary concern, with maintaining customer satisfaction as the ultimate goal. Toward this end, the framework of a customer relationship–building process should be to

1. establish channels and a procedure to accept customer communication;
2. through that communication identify what customers want and need;
3. then assess their levels of customer satisfaction; and,
4. accordingly, act on this customer communication and information.

RELATIONSHIP SELLING

Research suggests that not only do many firms not have a specific customer satisfaction program, which impacts the customer relationship–building process and the resulting outcomes, but most firms do not have a CAB or its equivalent, which can help track customer satisfaction levels and promote customer relationship building.

The ability to maintain relationships effectively is affected by *communicative competence,* which is the ability to perceive interpersonal relationships and adapt one's interaction goals and behaviors accordingly. Maintaining relationships involves the use of five strategies:

1. Positivity
2. Openness
3. Assurances
4. Sharing tasks
5. Social networks

Positivity, assurances, and sharing tasks predict relational commitment, satisfaction, and mutuality of control. A recent study by Marshall Prisbell at the University of Nebraska showed that individuals using strategies reflecting cooperation, cheerfulness, patience, and time to interface with another person rated themselves as showing warmth, empathy, composure, and social confirmation.[8]

Relationship selling, which is the process of bringing companies and their customers closer together, is a growing trend. Relationship selling involves getting customers to deal with a relationship-oriented person and neutralizing their expectation of being exploited. Whereas traditional selling is viewed as a contest with a winner and a loser and the sale is the end of the transaction, relationship selling is different; it is being friendly, professional, and service oriented so that follow-up is prioritized. Customers want to trust the salesperson, so listening and good communication are important.

With relationship selling, the sale is the beginning of building a relationship and customer loyalty. Customers feel more comfortable doing business with people they view as their friends, so it helps to develop such a bond with customers. To most effectively reach customers it is important to gain their trust because it is difficult to do business without it. Client trust allows better communications that can be used to help customers make buying decisions. With trust a customer will listen to the salesperson's suggestions and analysis more carefully. Creating customer loyalty through building is everyone's responsibility in the organization.

A CAB can assist in this process since the dynamics of a board actively improve the contact and dialogue that a company has with board members, who represent actual or prospective customers. Having customers involved as partners allows them to play a participatory role, enabling the company to see itself from the customers' standpoint, an invaluable insight.

Trust is developed not only through understanding but also when people respect similar values. Interpersonal trust is an essential aspect of healthy relationships. People must act in a trustworthy manner for trust to grow, and just as trusting behavior should increase trust, nontrusting actions should lead to its deterioration.[9] Trust building with customers entails

1. understanding, learning, and listening before selling;
2. asking focused, relevant questions;
3. being honorable and doing what you say you are going to do;
4. demonstrating to customers that you care about them; and
5. being able to relate to customers on their terms, in their language, and with respect for their value system.

Selling actually happens when people in the customer development effort build trust and focus on the customers' needs. This trust element may even cause customers to buy before they fully understand the product or service based on their belief that a company understands them and their problems.[10] Once clients become loyal they can also become advocates for the business, spreading positive "word of mouth" and referring their friends and business associates to a company.

The power of customer loyalty comes from repeat sales and increased market share. The actual face-to-face contact with customers and the feedback they provide can have great impact on measuring those product or service attributes most desired by customers. Effective salespeople have to be a valuable source of information and advice for clients, thereby promoting customer retention. CABs, by allowing companies to listen and keep in touch with their customers, are an effective way to build trust with customers. However, CABs should not be used to replace sales calls. They are instead a more formal customer interface sales tool that complements sales calls and provides industry and business information to keep both customers and companies out in front of their respective competition.

SUMMARY

The characteristics of a good board member are intelligence combined with business savvy and relevant industry experience and asking lots of focused questions to provide informed feedback on what a company is doing right and what it is doing wrong. An important factor in retaining board members is their having demonstrated the ability to learn and interact with fellow board members and company employees in a stimulating environment. The advisory board members should be composed of people who are not only business advisers but highly respected, people a firm would not want to let down. They are the group that a company can turn to for guidance and difficult decisions. These are the people who should embody the core values and standards to which the company aspires.

The successful companies of the twenty-first century will customize their products and services so they are tailored to individual customer preferences. To do this effectively, companies will have to learn a lot more about their customers. This will allow companies to get close enough to their customers to form friendships. This in turn will enable companies and customers to reach a level of mutual trust so that their destinies are almost interrelated.

Today's consumers know what they want and how much they are willing to pay. The sales force will not know what is important to a customer without asking, since it could be durability, faster service, better prices, warranties, easier financing, or any number of features. The delivery of value to the customer calls for a clear understanding of customer needs, superior product design, intelligent application of technology, focus on quality, cost control, productivity, and always finding the competitive edge. A CAB would seem to go to this purpose because dialogue with the board members allows for better communication with the marketplace as well as a way to build and strengthen relationships with customers. Most important for an effective sales effort is that CABs can enhance a firm's awareness of the needs of the marketplace and provide it with the opportunity to become a better company.[11]

CASE STUDY: SI CUSTOMER ADVISORY COUNCIL

Synopsis

SI Investments is a financial investments firm based in Cleveland, Ohio. The SI Customer Advisory Council was instituted in 1992. The meetings are run quarterly at the company's headquarters. Its original goals and objectives included "to share ideas and suggest ways that Company can improve programs and services to its customers."

Description

The SI Customer Council was brought in recently to help make business decisions. The council discussed assessment of late payment before it was implemented. It was recommended by the council to undertake a study of late-payment patterns and to research other utility policies regarding late payment. They suggested identifying special customers (disabled, elderly) and providing grace periods. They also gave suggestions on how to reduce late-paying customers by instituting electronic funds transfer (a very successful program today) and by promoting the level-billing plan. This met the critical role of the council, which is to help resolve strategies and make business decisions.

In addition, the council was influential in determining how to reach and improve customer service to non-English-speaking customers, a large customer segment of the SI community.

The council is also used as a tool to share ideas and information. The members "benefit personally and professionally from networking with each other." Although SI Customer Service sponsors the meetings, the members use them to share information about their own businesses. All members are given an opportunity to bring items to the meetings relating to their particular needs and upcoming events. At one meeting, the council was asked to lend their expertise in promoting and accomplishing a successful Business Networking Expo. The members offered valuable suggestions and commented that "they appreciated being able to discuss their issues and upcoming events. The members felt that sharing information with other council members enhanced a feeling of partnership" (Customer Outreach meeting notes). One member was able to save money by participating in the "time-of-use program."

Question

SI Investments is considering closing one of its Ohio business offices. What role can the SI Customer Advisory Council play in this decision?

APPENDIX: CAB SURVEY RESULTS

Has your customer advisory board helped your customer relationship–building process? Please explain why or why not and where you hold these meetings.

- Distributor council meetings are held to review issues/concerns associated with distributor sales and how to support their efforts.
- Surgeons actually review and approve all new products during the development phase. It is very valuable in that it validates products in a clinical setting.
- All of our accounts are managed by relationship managers who oversee and manage the total relationship. They tell us that we should earn *x* amount of money based on capital usage of our balance sheet.
- The advisory board is comprised of "internal customers"—territory managers. This is intended to be an opportunity to hear them and bring them up to speed on our direction and progress. Resort areas are used as locations. This is a three-year term and a position of honor.
- Customer feedback, i.e., new areas of business, is the focus.
- First meeting was held at corporate headquarters; subsequent meetings may be held in different parts of North America to minimize travel/maximize leisure activities.
- Customers provide feedback on usage of products.
- Meetings are in a different location every year (only three years thus far).
- Meetings are held in Paris/Houston. The board adds great value to client relationship and development of technology.
- Weekly meetings are held with groups of key suppliers.
- The board is used for joint technology development to ensure that new technology products will satisfy client needs.
- Board members are usually taken to a nice place outside of the city, all expenses paid, sometimes with their spouses.
- Industry meetings are held in the corporate office.

If your customers were unable to attend any customer advisory board meetings, were there any particular reasons why?

- Typically scheduling conflict—a lead time of three to four months helpful in avoiding this
- Travel Budget International customers—budget constraints
- Not to my knowledge
- Well attended
- Typically would expect attendance except for dire emergencies

- Good attendance
- Usually company policies against accepting invitations from suppliers or vendors

When you conduct customer advisory board meetings, how is the meeting agenda developed?

- By our president, focusing on current industry issues that face our customers and affect our product use; new product manufacture and/or changes; research and development (R&D)
- From marketing, sales; R&D objectives set based on known use of product
- Social mainly—minimal time spent discussing business in a formal meeting
- Initially by regional managers, with future meetings a collective collaborative effort
- Feedback from distributors focused on common issues
- Surgeon as chairperson who approves topics recommended by all parties
- By/with product development directed by president of sales
- Agenda developed 75 percent based on company interests, 25 percent based on customer interests
- By product development and sales
- Joint effort between customers and sales organization

When you conduct customer advisory board meetings, who leads and moderates these meetings?

- President
- Vice president of sales and marketing director
- Vice president/managing director
- President/CEO and vice president of sales; managers from all functional groups
- Senior banker followed by a product specialist
- Other surgeons and product development people
- Distribution manager
- Director of product development

What suggestions would you give your company on "how to successfully sell" their various products?

- Initiate a shift to consultative approach.
- Establish a focus group by industry.

- "Listen" to managers and continue to provide a good mix from marketing and technology.
- Listen to the customer: What keeps the customer up at night? Solve that problem.
- Develop relationships with customers—know their needs.
- Sell value added.
- Apply knowledge; develop customer intimacy.
- Treat more customer involvement as a plus.
- See more solutions rather than products and services.
- Add resources, more training.
- Establish long-term business plans based on product life cycles.
- Improve competency.

What suggestions, concerns, or complaints do you have, if any, about your firm's products or how you operate as a company?

- We need a greater systems solution approach to selling, not just an individual product.
- We need technical assistance.
- We need improved communication between sales and business units—align these; response to market needs is too slow to introduce new products.
- Our customers operate on a global basis, and when they use our services they want the same "face" and price globally.
- The future is coming fast; we are not always quick to respond or better lead.
- Most are old products.
- We have a limited product line and approval/application for these products—extend product line; gain approval for new indications.
- We have no stock option/equity opportunity.
- We need to have more of a sales focus.

What do your customers consider to be the most important attributes in people whom they actually deal with at your firm?

- Knowledgeable (in product application and industry)
- Consistent quality
- Clinical aspect that our products offer patients
- Product knowledge, reliability, resourcefulness
- Expertise, morality
- Trust and technical competence in field and application; follow-through from our customer service group
- Accountability, price, and material knowledge

- Relationships, value, and consistency in service
- Professionalism
- Service, product knowledge, and industry knowledge
- Technically competent and consultative style
- Interpersonal skills, understanding customer needs
- Service oriented, respectful, knowledgeable, good communication skills, good business skills

In your opinion, if you had to point to the top five future trends in your own business, what would they be?

- New methods of product distribution via channels
- More aggressive competition via financial initiatives
- Technology advancement
- Alliances
- E-commerce
- Increased pricing pressure
- Service demands
- Demographics shifting to secondary markets
- Smaller sales force (management)
- Price cuts, specifically by government
- Sales expansion
- Risk/reward sharing
- Value-added relationships
- More innovation
- Education
- Increased overseas competition—China, India

If you had to point to the top five qualifications of the ideal business contact or salesperson profile that your company would have, what would they be?

- Relationship focused
- Service oriented
- Trustworthy
- Tenacity
- Market experience
- Professional sales representative—not a greenhorn
- Proven technological experience
- Knowledge in product development
- Empathy
- Technically oriented

- Smart
- Good business skills
- Integrity
- Experience
- Dedicated/reliable
- Organizational skills, use of time, follow-up

Other Survey Questions and Results

Figures 1.3 through 1.7 graphically depict companies' views of how CABs have affected their business practices.

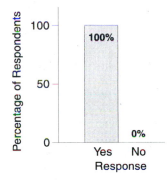

FIGURE 1.3. Do you think that there will be an increase in the amount of business that you expect to do in the next three years? (*Source:* Carter Customer Advisory Board Survey, 2002.)

FIGURE 1.4. How would you assess client satisfaction regarding the technical knowledge of your staff related to the products or services that they sell, as discussed at customer advisory board meetings? (*Source:* Carter Customer Advisory Board Survey, 2002.)

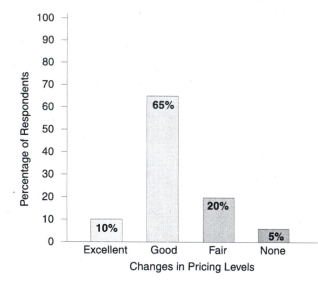

FIGURE 1.5. How would you assess any changes in your pricing levels as a result of discussions at a customer advisory board meeting? (*Source:* Carter Customer Advisory Board Survey, 2002.)

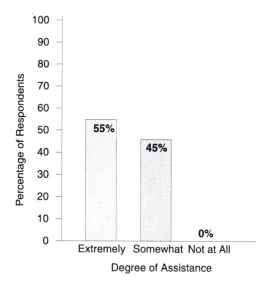

FIGURE 1.6. Has your customer advisory board helped your customer relationship building? (*Source:* Carter Customer Advisory Board Survey, 2002.)

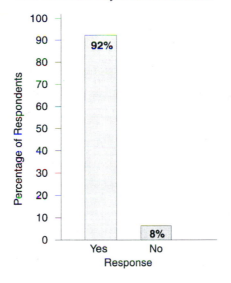

FIGURE 1.7. Does your firm do a good job of customer relationship building with your clients? (*Source:* Carter Customer Advisory Board Survey, 2002.)

Chapter 2

The Customer Relationship–Building Process

The customer asset management approach has been referred to as "relationship marketing," and the focus of most research studies has been the relationships among channel members. However, the perspective that customers are an asset to be managed is applicable to a broad range of customer relationships. One type that is receiving increased research attention is the area of membership relationships.

Despite the plethora of membership programs developed by organizations and the pervasiveness of memberships acquired and maintained by individuals, little academic study focuses on the management of memberships. One study surveyed art museum members and found that the major correlates of a member's organizational identification are the prestige associated with membership in the museum and the length of membership. Another study found that membership length, donating, and involvement in related interest groups reduce the likelihood of lapsed memberships.

CUSTOMER SELLING MODES
AND MEMBERSHIP COMMITMENT

Customers now seek three selling modes (see Box 2.1). The first of these modes, *transactional sales*, occurs when purchasers already

---

BOX 2.1. Customer Selling Modes

- Transactional Sales → Intrinsic Value
- Consultative Sales → Extrinsic Value
- Enterprise Sales → Strategic Value

---

have a full understanding of their needs and the products and services they intend to buy. As a result, they do not truly need the services of a salesperson. The second mode, *consultative sales,* arises when buyers do not have this kind of extensive knowledge of the market and their own needs. They depend upon the salesperson to help them determine their needs and match available products and services to those needs in the most cost-effective manner. The third mode, *enterprise sales,* is appropriate for very large business-to-business sales and requires that the strategic interests of customer and supplier be aligned. The object of this relationship is to create value: the customer uses the salesperson and the selling organization as a partner or strategic ally.[1]

It is absolutely necessary for a sales force in today's complex selling environment to understand the customer's desired selling mode. Without that understanding, it becomes impossible to service the customer effectively and allocate corporate resources to meet customer needs in such a way as to provide satisfaction. In other words, if a customer were in the transactional selling mode, having a salesperson call on that account would be an inefficient allocation of a corporation's sales resources. Moreover, it would have a negative effect on the customer that could result in a lost sale.

The driving force in contemporary sales is the idea of value creation. *Intrinsic value creation* involves customers who buy for product value alone and perceive little value in the selling effort itself. A customer who views a purchase in this manner would most likely pursue a transactional selling mode. With *extrinsic value creation,* buyers look for value from the sales effort and pursue the consultative selling mode. The final type of customer, compatible with *strategic value creation,* leverages suppliers' competencies and assesses them as potential partners, rather than merely as potential suppliers of a product or service.

The general definition of membership commitment is the degree of the member's psychological attachment to the association. *Continuance commitment,* which is based on the self-interest stake in a relationship, is defined as the degree to which the member is psychologically bonded to the organization on the basis of the perceived costs (economic, social, and status related) associated with leaving the organization. In contrast, we define *normative commitment,* which derives from a person's sense of moral obligation to maintain the relationship with the organization. Finally, *affective commitment* is focused on a positive emotional attachment and is the degree to which the member is psychologically bonded to the organization on the basis of how favorable he or she feels toward the organization.[2]

Linking Commitment with Behavioral Outcomes

Organizational behavior research provides support for a positive relationship among the three dimensions of commitment and retention, linking the affective view of commitment with a member's involvement in the organization. Therefore, higher levels of affective commitment are hypothesized to lead to higher levels of participation. Affective commitment is also hypothesized to affect coproduction. People who are committed to the organization are willing to give something of themselves to promote the organization's well-being.

Member interdependence enhancement is defined as the extent to which the organization provides its members with the motivation, opportunity, and ability to exchange value with one another. Marketers who are interested in building relationships with their customers must address the ways they help their customers build productive relationships among themselves (i.e., enhancing the interdependence among their customers). For example, Winer and colleagues note the importance of customer interaction in the formation of brand-based Internet communities, explaining that customers' interactions during periods of waiting in line have an influence on the level of customer satisfaction. Interdependence among members is becoming increasingly managerially relevant in the rapidly expanding world of online services (e.g., America Online, Yahoo) because the interactive networks for special interests and bulletin boards are among the more frequently used services. These networks depend on interaction among the users' members. With regard to associations, research conducted by the National Association of Insurance and Financial Advisors (NAIFA) reveals that one of the consistently highest-rated benefit of being a member of the association was the ability to network with other members. The task for the relationship marketer is to set up the best systems, environment, and supportive personnel to facilitate this process.[3]

Member interdependence enhancement is hypothesized to affect directly two forms of commitment: continuance and normative. Enhancing the interdependence among members is expected to have a positive effect on continuance commitment because it raises the cost of exiting the relationship with the organization of interest. In addition to losing the benefits directly controlled by the organization, members no longer receive the considerable advantages (e.g., job-related information, professional contacts) they derive from their relationships with others from the cohort or in-group. Enhancing members' interdependence is expected to affect normative commitment positively for two reasons. First, increasing these interdependencies results in these members developing obligations to others in the group. Second, through their interactions with others, they develop a sense of belonging. Therefore, these members develop a strong belief that they ought to remain in the organization so as not to abandon the other members.

Dissemination of Organizational Knowledge

Increasing its knowledge of the customer, or, as is popularly stated, "getting close to the customer," is a key ingredient in an organization's attempts to provide value to its customers. A complementary but often overlooked task of relationship marketing involves "getting the customer closer to the organization." The process of *organizational socialization*—the way members adapt to and come to appreciate the values, norms, and behavior patterns of an organization—captures the essence of this task. Dissemination of organizational knowledge is a means of enhancing the socialization of members. Such distribution of information to the membership includes the organization's goals and values; its culture; and its politics, processes, and personnel—three content areas that are central to the socialization of organizational members. Comprehension of the organization's goals and values helps link the membership to the mission of the organization as a whole, and knowledge of the culture of the organization provides guidelines regarding appropriate behaviors expected of the membership. Members' awareness of the politics, processes, and personnel of the organization helps members operate more efficiently in the organizational relationship.[4]

Organizational behavior research has theorized (though not empirically tested) that organizational knowledge will have a positive effect on members' normative commitment. Members who better understand the linkages between the goals and values of the organization and how they affect the industry from which the members derive their living experience an enhanced sense of normative commitment because of the interdependent nature of these goals. Similarly, this research proposes that the antecedents of affective commitment are based on experiences that fulfill members' psychological needs to feel comfortable and competent in the roles they play within the organization. Exploratory interviews show that a lack of relevant information keeps members on the fringe of the group.

Marketers also can enhance relationships by providing an environment that promotes the members' motivation, opportunity, and ability to create value among themselves. In addition to providing regular opportunities for members to exchange value face-to-face, associations can benefit from the development of a Web site. Here, the members can interact with one another on the basis of their common interests. Customer interdependence is becoming an increasingly important issue to marketers across industries, as many customer groups or communities are beginning to form and interact through Web sites on the Internet. For example, when SPSS, Inc., President and Chief Executive Officer Jack Noonan announced his company's Web site, he stated, "In addition to providing the latest information on our company and products, our web site gives SPSS users everywhere an open forum for the exchange of ideas and usage tips that can help them get the most out of data analysis tools." Organizations that seek to develop and manage Web communities can benefit from studying the ways that associations have successfully brought people together around a common cause or interest.[5]

Enhancing Buyer-Supplier Relationships

The business marketing and channel management literature has been paying increasing attention to understanding the benefits of building closer buyer-supplier relationships. Most of the research has focused on explaining how relational processes lead to outcomes such as cooperation, satisfaction, trust, and commitment. Recently, business practitioners have sought to quantify the value that might be derived from efficient management of buyer-supplier relationships. Buying firms are paying more attention to working with suppliers that deliver value by helping lower a customer firm's costs. Given that 56 percent of the average manufacturing firm's budget is spent on materials, a buying firm may realize significant opportunities for cost savings by identifying suppliers that behave in ways which help lower the customer firm's costs.

Three types of customer costs are prominently discussed as being affected by supplier relationships: (1) direct product costs (price), (2) acquisition costs, and (3) operations costs. *Direct product costs* are the actual prices charged by the supplier for the main products sold to a customer firm. Because these costs are the most easily measured, they traditionally have received the most attention from business buyers and sellers. *Acquisition costs* are those which customers incur in acquiring and storing products from a particular supplier. They include expenses related to ordering, delivering, and storing products, as well as the expense of monitoring supplier performance and coordinating and communicating with the supplier. Lowering such costs has been the primary objective of the supply chain management movement in purchasing and logistics practices. *Operations costs* are inherent in the customer firm's primary business. In the manufacturing context, such costs include expenses for research and development, manufacturing and downtime, and internal coordination. The quality movement and activity-based costing have directed attention to the ability of supplier relationships to affect these expenses. Together, direct product, acquisition, and operations costs form the total customer firm costs affected by supplier relationships.[6]

Ultimately, the continuation of the trend toward more collaborative business relationships will be based on the ability of such relationships to generate demonstrable value to the participants. Although value can be created in many ways, one of the primary and most practical objectives is to lower total cost in the value chain. Effective cost management provides firms with a significant source of competitive advantage, and several emerging business marketing practices aim to lower total system costs (e.g., supply chain management, efficient consumer response, quick response, just-in-time inventory management).

DEFINING THE CUSTOMER
RELATIONSHIP SALES PROCESS

The sales process is a practical and actionable expression of the sales strategy (see Figure 2.1). It provides end-to-end guidance on

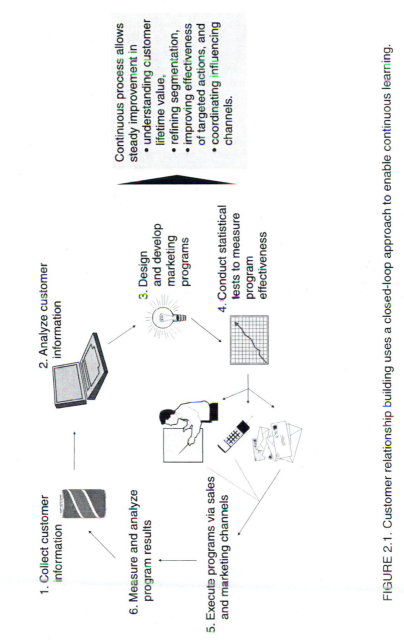

1. Collect customer information

2. Analyze customer information

3. Design and develop marketing programs

4. Conduct statistical tests to measure program effectiveness

5. Execute programs via sales and marketing channels

6. Measure and analyze program results

Continuous process allows steady improvement in
- understanding customer lifetime value,
- refining segmentation,
- improving effectiveness of targeted actions, and
- coordinating influencing channels.

FIGURE 2.1. Customer relationship building uses a closed-loop approach to enable continuous learning.

how all the players in the sales engine engage with the customer and with one another. It is a set of discrete, progressive phases that describe what a firm does with a customer to move from first contact to first sale and on through successive stages of resale and cross sale. It identifies the various components of a complete sales cycle, along with specific qualification criteria and suggested strategies, tactics, and countertactics to be utilized. It incorporates tools and messages to be provided to all business development personnel, who are then equipped with a common language to facilitate internal communications. The key is the ability both to discern the decisive point and to engage the right resources at the right time to secure the sale, deployment, and use of your offer, ultimately leading to total customer satisfaction.

The essential purpose of a sales process is to deliver a branded customer experience (which should also include the provision of unique products and services). Branding is predicated on owning a position in the mind of the customer. This claim to ownership is driven by four factors:

1. *Differentiation:* This is the engine. The customer must perceive that the offer, company, solution, etc., are truly different from the other viable alternatives.
2. *Relevance:* Difference alone does not get it done. The brand must also be relevant and appropriate to the customer's sensibility, value system, ability to adopt innovation, etc.
3. *Esteem:* The customer must admire and respect the brand and the related deliverables.
4. *Knowledge:* The customer actually has to know about the brand—though too much knowledge can be a dangerous thing. If they think they know everything, new knowledge falls on deaf ears.

Customers are tired of empty promises. Every customer-facing activity needs to hold the promise of added value or you risk losing the customer's commitment, interest, and, ultimately, attention. The value to the customer cannot just occur when he or she buys and uses your product, service, or solution. Instead, the sales process, and by extension all customer contact people, must replace touting, demonstrating, and comparing products or services with behaviors and activities that the customer perceives as valuable. This is especially true for sellers because the burden for demonstrating immediate value is so much greater.[7]

The final process should be expanded to integrate sales behaviors (activities and skills), sales tools, sales and marketing support, coaching and management behaviors, coaching tools, coaching process, partnering, solution configuration and fulfillment, and information technology.

METHODS TO BUILD CUSTOMER RELATIONSHIPS

One of the most valuable tools that marketing can provide to the sales team is a standardized set of compelling business messages that identifies the value the firm can deliver to create interest with prospects' senior managers and executives; these are usually called *value messages* or *value propositions*. If sellers do not have target market information (see Box 2.2 and Figure 2.2) or standardized sales tools directed at this market, then one of two things will happen:

1. They will try to come up with a tool for their own use.
2. They will simply go without a tool and wing it each time, which results in suboptimized performance.

Competitive Market Analysis

Competitive advantage is the holy grail of marketing, and yet too often the best competitive insights and weapons fail to appear in an immediately useful form for use by the sales team. In fact, often, sell-

---

BOX 2.2. Understanding the Target Market

- *What is market segmentation?*
  Market segmentation is the process of dividing the total, heterogeneous market for a product into several submarkets or segments, each of which tends to be homogeneous in all significant aspects, e.g., region, age, sex, and ethnicity.
- *What are the important elements of competition analysis?*
  Staff, philosophy, geographic scope, products, financial condition, location, distinctive advantage.

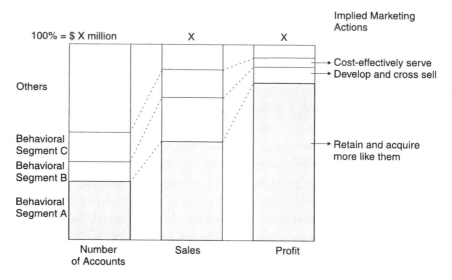

FIGURE 2.2. Customer relationship building is based on segmentation and targeted marketing. (*Note:* Customer segmentation identifies profit concentration; $ in millions, percent.)

ers are left to devise their own competitive strategies, relying on price concessions, lengthy product demo cycles, exhausting proposal-writing marathons, and lots of haggling and negotiating to ward off the competition and get the deal done. Many purchasing departments will wait until the closing days of the quarter (or year) to start serious negotiations, knowing full well that companies will make all sorts of concessions to get their business.

Marketing must take the lead in collecting, analyzing, and disseminating competitive intelligence for utilization at the point of sale. To do this properly, they need to get as close to the customer and the field as possible (see Table 2.1). (In addition to more typical research methods, marketing can gain some of its best competitive information from conducting win/loss sessions with both the sales team and the customer/prospect personnel.) Although marketing is the leader in this activity, it must be a two-way information exchange between sales and marketing in order to be successful.[8]

Marketing can also bring tremendous value to the sales team by producing competitive playbooks, in which the strategies and tactics of common competitors are recounted (sometimes predicted), and then countertactics and counterstrategies are recommended.

TABLE 2.1. Customer relationship building uses customer information to create and deepen customer relationships.

Definition	Key Attributes
Customer relationship building is a companywide customer management approach that uses prospective and existing customer information to take targeted actions that increase the number and value of customer relationships.	• *Value based*—actions driven by view of current and potential value of individual customers • *Segmentation driven*—uses actual customers and prospect behaviors and other characteristics to create actionable segments for targeted, tailored, and timed marketing programs • *Multiple channels*—sales and service conducted through the channel that is simultaneously most efficient and most likely to yield the best results • *Closed-loop process*—requires ongoing testing, tracking, and evaluation of programs, customer interactions, and customer segments to drive continuous learning and improvement • *Integrated*—requires cooperation between multiple business functions to engineer and link each step in the customer management process • *IT enabled*—uses a variety of information technologies to capture, analyze, and manage customer information across the organization

Before Transactions

What sort of presales support does a sales team need? Depending on your go-to-market sales strategy, this could be as simple as the provision of preformatted forms, templates, and guidelines or as complex as a phalanx of attorneys, financial analysts, contract specialists, technical analysts, and systems engineers. Fulfillment needs to provide the sales team with clear expectations, investment guidelines, cost models and assumptions, service level agreements (SLAs), escalation procedures, etc., for requesting and deploying proper levels of support. They must define a process to provide sellers with quick input into customer-requested modifications or customizations.[9]

The inverse of each of these points is true: fulfillment does not own all of the responsibility for presales support. Decisions as to what capabilities are important to customers and the market at large are a shared role across the sales machine (see Figure 2.3). Those capabilities which meet or exceed customer needs and desires, as well as those which can create differentiation or competitive advantage, need to be identified, shared, and supported. Customers and competitors continually raise the bar on expectations and requirements, and the challenge is not only to surpass the bar but to keep everyone on the sales team at the same level.

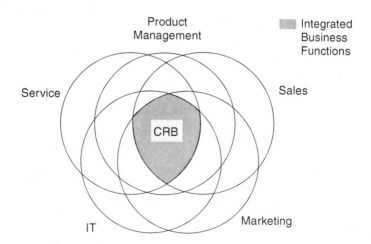

FIGURE 2.3. Successful customer relationship building is integrated and requires coordination among many functions.

Fulfillment must also take responsibility for measuring and monitoring customer value and satisfaction and disseminating insight back through the organization. The customers' perception of the value they received is all that really matters for repeat business. There are numerous ways of capturing customer satisfaction metrics beyond the obvious satisfaction surveys and client visits, including regularly measuring, tracking, and communicating fulfillment's performance in regard to the delivery and service guidelines and expectations noted earlier.

MAINTAINING CUSTOMER RELATIONSHIPS AND THE CAB

Hardly a single person in business does not know that keeping and expanding a customer relationship is far less expensive and far more profitable than going to the market to develop a new customer, take one from a competitor, or win one back that has recently been lost.

The life of a customer relationship has many *moments of truth.* Among the most important are those which immediately follow the first sale, when expectations are high and the sales team is exhausted. Many large sales are stolen away in the early stages by a savvy competitor who watches and waits for the all too inevitable early disappointments.

In other cases, the pivotal moment appears every three years:

- You win the business in the first year based on a brilliant presentation and promises of fabulous things to come.
- You transfer your best people off the account to pursue other new business, or, worse, because you can't make money based on the contract you signed in year one.
- The perceived value is delivered in years one and two.
- The business goes back out for bid in year three amid dashed hopes and finger-pointing between client and provider.

Brilliant execution and customer service can make up for many other performance weaknesses along the way. Still, perhaps no other area holds as much potential for severely damaging the company's market reputation than the negative repercussions from misalignment and missed commitments in these areas.[10]

In today's competitive field of business, a few concepts must be understood for a business to be successful. In the field of sales, the most important business function is not how fast you can create a new product or how many items you can turn out in a single day. It is much simpler than that. You can have the greatest product or idea in the world, but if you do not have any customers, your business is headed for failure.

The most important facet in sales is customer relationship building (see Box 2.3). It is very important that your customers feel that they are wanted and respected and not just seen as a revenue-earning opportunity for you. Once you have established a client base, you must keep up a friendly relationship with them. A large percentage of your annual earnings will be from repeat sales and referral business.[11]

It is also a good idea to know what your clients want. This is where the economic idea of supply and demand comes into play. It does not make any sense to offer a product that people do not want. To keep their clients' best interests in mind, many companies, especially start-ups, turn to the CAB, to gain insight into rapidly changing markets. CABs can be very helpful in getting a business off the ground. They provide a company with knowledge and insight and facilitate entry into a particular field. A board consisting of future clients is one way to nearly ensure a successful business.

Customer or technical advisory boards are usually formed as follows: Once the firm has developed an idea for a product, it first figures out what companies it would most like to have as customers, or its target market. Next, the firm invites one or two key decision makers from each of these businesses to sit on the advisory board. To ensure the board members' full cooperation and interest the firm may offer members $10,000 to $40,000 in stock options. Now it is time to build a relationship with them through phone contacts, brainstorming, lunches, and e-mail updates.[12]

When the product is finished and ready for the market, the firm uses board members to gain entry into the target market companies through introductions to other key decision makers. If everything goes as planned, the firm makes sales to these companies and the business is on its way to success. Maintaining good customer relationships will enable continuing business with these companies and may even lead to referral business. Thus, CABs benefit both board members, by giving them stock options, and companies, by giving them a client base.

BOX 2.3. Customer Relationship Building

- *What is it?*
  A commitment to develop a rapport with customers and provide a valuable service through that relationship.
- *What should be done to begin building?*
  Sale is the beginning of building loyalty and trust with clients. Here, selling is getting customers to deal with a relationship-oriented person.
- *What can firms do to develop relationships?*
  Relationship selling—listening to clients, emphasizing a service orientation, and prioritizing follow-up.
- *What helps to maintain relationships?*
  Establishing a procedure to accept customer communication; identifying what customers desire and the satisfaction they derive from the relationship; acting on customer communication.

Objectives

- Customer relationship building is certainly necessary.
- Effective customer relationship building allows a company to treat customers as individuals, understand and anticipate their needs, and tailor products and services to meet those needs.
- Customer relationship–building initiatives are complex and consist of dozens of interrelated goals and projects under a single umbrella.

Reasons for Failure

- Organizational change and politics
- Lack of the right skills and enterprisewide understanding of the initiatives
- Poor planning
- Unable to manage change effectively

CAB Advantages and Disadvantages

CABs have an upside and a downside. The old saying "One hand washes the other" is very relevant when it comes to CABs. A top executive will help your company by sitting on your company's advisory board. He or she will give you input and feedback on whatever you ask. With his or her help your company may become a Fortune

500 business. In return, your business will give this board member stock options.[13] Your company can make a lot of money depending on who is on your board, and your board members can make a lot of money off of the success of the company.

Jim McManus retired last year as vice president and lead systems engineer of UUNET, a subsidiary of MCI WorldCom and operator of the world's largest Internet backbone. McManus retired with a personal fortune of over $20 million. Most of his wealth did not come from his work with UUNET, but from the stocks he received from sitting on various advisory boards. He sat on at least three advisory boards with networking equipment companies such as Avici Systems, Sycamore Networks, and Redstone Communications. Along with the shares he received from them because of his help on their boards, he also bought shares as a private investor.

Another CAB perk that led to his $20 million fortune is that he was granted friend and family shares, which are options that a CEO hands out just before a company's initial public offering. If the share prices go wild after the initial public offering, the holders of the friend and family shares receive a nice windfall.

Another tool used to lure big-time executives onto an advisory board, besides the stock options, is to treat them to a round of golf at an elite country club or luxury box seats at a major sporting event. Although they are illegal, bribes are also used to gain the interest of possible advisory board candidates.

The practice of advisory boards is so common in the networking equipment industry that two-thirds of all start-up companies have them, with customers or potential customers as members. Start-up companies generally prefer to have members from big companies on their boards. Large telecommunications companies spend billions of dollars on equipment to build huge networks. If you have one of these powerhouses on your advisory board, chances are they will place a huge order. Last year Sycamore Networks went public with a $12 billion valuation and the company had only one customer: Williams Communications, which is building an ultramodern high-speed data network.

Some big-name executives with such companies as Lucent, Nortek Cisco, and Ciena do not support the way new businesses use their advisory boards to get their clients. Others view advisory boards as nothing more than marketing ploys to impress venture capitalists, customers, and investment bankers. Many CEOs sign up for these boards and never attend meetings. Gautam Prakash, a former partner with Bessemer Venture Partners, notes, "Most of them don't add much value. Partially because management teams don't utilize them, and partially because there is not much commitment by the board members."[14] In addition, some people think that having advisory boards is not good business ethics. They believe that by forming these boards businesses are buying their customers.[15]

CASE STUDY: SALES FORCE TRANSITION, PG INDUSTRIES, INC.

Synopsis

The sales force with the PG business has traditionally been highly technically competent with relatively low commercial skills or interactions. There is a more senior group in place today, with needed transition and evolution due over the next eighteen to twenty-four months.

Background

PG's business supplies fiberglass yarn to the electronics industry for the ultimate manufacture of circuit boards, as well as to a multitude of different specialty businesses for use in such products as reinforced tape, insect screening, medical casting, cement backer board, etc.

The sales force for North America includes four account managers, who report to me. Accounts are segregated based on market use and somewhat on geography. Three of the account managers are seasoned PG fiberglass account veterans, with a combined eighty years of experience in fiberglass industries. They have a high level of knowledge relative to our customers and our customers' processes, but a relatively low level of knowledge of downstream markets and value. Over the years they have been somewhat shielded from commercial issues, especially pricing negotiations.

Problem Headline

Sales force transition will occur over the next eighteen to twenty-four months in terms of people, such that a robust process of training, skill development, and changed focus needs to be established and implemented shortly. The current organization is not properly prepared to deal with changes in the industry.

Description

This business has evolved from being 80 percent electronic and 20 percent specialty to being approximately 50/50 in terms of customer base and sales. This is being driven by the industry, as well as PG's strategic decision to build a better electronics/specialty mix over the past three to five years. At the same time, we have evolved through personalities, from being very closed in our handling of sensitive customer interactions (i.e., the business general manager was the only one who negotiated prices with key customers), to being more open internally and driving decision making and accountability down to our account managers. Our previous handling of these situations has taught our account managers to deal only with technical issues and to avoid many sensitive commercial issues, such as price. In addition, in the past, we jumped through hoops whenever our customers asked us to and subsequently ended up with a huge variety of products with only slight differences from one another. Product proliferation has festered for many years. Commercial issues associated with trying to change this approach are very difficult for our account managers to deal with directly.

We recognize that with retirements planned over the next two years, we will have an issue with consistency within the handling of our customer base, and the loss of an enormous amount of talent and experience. At the same time, though, we recognize this as an opportunity to make fundamental changes in our sales approach if we can come up with the right transition process.

Another issue that we face is the segmenting of our customer base. Our account managers are currently segmented somewhat by geography, but mainly by customer prices. This has been the most convenient way to handle this over time. We have flexibility, since three of our account managers are in North Carolina (where the lion's share of our customer base is) and the fourth is in Pittsburgh.

Questions

- What are the pros/cons of different customer-segmenting approaches?
- Sales force transition: Is it better to set up ongoing transitions and manage for forced turnover or to create stability to address keeping the customer comfortable with his or her PG contract without a lot of turnover?
- We need advice on dealing with changing someone's view of his or her value to the sales organization after being rewarded for handling his or her job a certain way for thirty years. Is a different incentive/compensation system an alternative to address this?

Chapter 3

Customer Focus

The aim of a customer focus strategy is to examine the provision of products and services to customers that are perceived by customers to be of greater value than they could expect to receive from the competition in similar markets (see Box 3.1). Indeed, the competitive advantage provided by the application of a strategy for creating customer value provides not only continuous improvement in business processes and operational effectiveness but also the competitive intelligence by which strategic planning can bring about increased market share (see Box 3.2).[1]

When customers perceive that the value they receive from the supplier is higher relative to what they can receive from competitors, they remain loyal to their service provider and the likelihood of repeat business is significantly increased. "Getting it right" with customers is the key to success. In fact, it is important to achieve greater than a 50 percent satisfaction level because performance at that level means that only 50 percent of customers are likely to remain loyal and provide repeat orders. This translates into something quite startling: *customers are equally likely to buy from competitors in the future.* Customer loyalty comes from having a customer value management strategy that provides

- a focus on the customer's perception of value rather than the supplier's perception;
- identification of the key purchase criteria and attributes of the customer and their importance to the customer; and
- segmentation of customer needs into actionable parts that are linked to internal processes, such as customer account improvement plans.

BOX 3.1. Customer Focus Strategy

Mission Statement

To develop a policy and strategy that establishes customer focus as an integral part of the operating plan for all lines of business.

Vision Statement

Make a company where all associates support one another, customers, and vendors in ways that their "unique" characteristics become enablers of, rather than barriers to, corporate success and increased shareholder value.

Customer Commitment

- *With associates*
  We are committed to creating awareness and understanding of customer needs and differences. We will work together, with respect and dignity, to build a proactive and adaptive organization.
- *With customers*
  We are committed to capitalizing on the qualities that associates and suppliers bring to the workplace, to maximize our ability to develop innovative solutions to serve our customer base. We will work together with customers to exceed their expectations.
- *With suppliers*
  We are committed to supplier diversity, offering increased business opportunities and bringing better solutions to our customers. We will work together to build a supplier base that provides competitive advantage.
- *With the communities we serve*
  We are committed to corporate citizenship and being good corporate citizens. We will work together to honor every community we touch.

The aim of a CAB is to get extremely close to customers. Many businesses "get it wrong" when trying to launch a new product or service; all they do is try to imagine what the customer's response will be when face-to-face with the service or product being offered. Instead of asking the customer's advice, or even watching what the customer does and trying to understand from that what the customer wants, most businesses simply take calculated guesses.

BOX 3.2. Strategic Customer Focus to Enhance Shareholder Value

- *Externally, for business growth, market penetration, and profitability*
  Improve market share and market penetration
  Know the customer base
  Brand (advertising and promotion of services)
- *Internally, for attraction and retention of talent*
  Promote workplace effectiveness
  Encourage learning/innovating through diverse perspectives
- *Both internally and externally through innovation*

The key to success lies not in guessing but in knowing, understanding, and giving clients what they want. A CAB is one of the most effective ways to develop strategic customer focus (see Box 3.3) to find out what customers want. Companies need to find out how to get more customers like the best 20 percent and how to keep them coming back. The first two ways are to increase the number of desired customers and to increase their frequency of business dealings.

In running a CAB, companies can either meet with different customers from a target sector each time or meet with the same customers over and over again. The first option has the advantage of providing new insights during each meeting. A difficulty with the second option is getting the same customers to give continually the benefit of their time. Sharing plans and strategies with customers at CABs provides invaluable information about their attitudes and beliefs that can lead to a successful customer focus strategy.

Senior executives need to make market focus a personal, strategic priority to initiate organizational change. Most top-level managers routinely spend time visiting customers, but frequently these visits are superficial, and the managers do not invest the effort needed to understand and empathize with the customer. Top-level managers need to spend a day in the life of key customers in their business processes. There is no substitute for managers' instincts, imagination, and personal knowledge of the market.[2] Treating customers and shareholders with honesty and respect is a good start if a company really wants to improve service.[3] Companies depend on customers for their existence, but businesses are often organized for their own

BOX 3.3. Strategic Customer Focus

Customer Advisory Board Vision

- Make a company that truly values customers and where all associates support one another, customers, and vendors in ways that their unique characteristics become enablers of, rather than barriers to, corporate success and increase shareholder value

Customer Focus Strategic Plans

- Marketplace is changing dramatically—Global expansion and deregulation
- Organizational structure is evolving—Creation of operating units and consolidation of corporate services
- How can a customer focus help position a company for long-term success?

Action-Learning Component

- Approach
  Build a customer focus business case for PSEG and operating companies through a series of action-learning workshops
  Provide a framework for how a customer focus can and should be incorporated into the business strategy/planning process
  Establish and implement an action-learning process whereby business planners jointly develop a framework to be used in future business planning
- Expected outcomes
  A roadmap for a comprehensive, coordinated, and consistent customer focus strategy
  Clear alignment of customer focus strategy with business objectives
  Increased capacity of business strategists/planners to use and apply a "leveraging customer focus lens" in their planning processes
  Organizational action plans defining steps to implement the customer focus strategy

Specific Actions Under Way

- Series of action-learning workshops under development to build strategic customer focus business case
- Customer focus Web site under development
- Customer focus training—"managing customers" and efficacy seminars

convenience rather than the customer's. CABs employed in companies' reengineering efforts help make companies truly customer focused.[4]

Reengineering is something that should be used primarily for major processes that play a significant role, such as customer service or sales activity. Effective reengineering looks at doing things most effectively and asks the following questions:

What are our core competencies?
Where should we compete?
What is our distinctive advantage?
How do our customers define value?
What changes should we make to adjust to developments in the marketplace?

The key focus with reengineering is to work on the process. The threat of instituting changes is the possibility of job losses, but the necessity of changing due to competitive and marketplace forces can dictate the need for urgent changes. Positioning to face these challenges in the form of good leadership, enhanced skills, and team involvement is necessary. The result, if successful, is achievement and empowerment. A strategic approach to reengineering involves defining goals and the business process; listening to customers; benchmarking; using tools such as technology, where appropriate; developing a reengineering plan of action; and monitoring and evaluating outcomes.

CUSTOMERS AND REENGINEERING

Managers can play an essential role during reengineering by bringing the customer into the process. Radical changes in the business environment have dictated the need for reengineering in organizations. These changes in the marketplace have involved developments such as technology, sophisticated customers, globalization, company mergers and acquisitions, rising business and sales costs, impact of the quality movement, communication volume and speed, and the need for adaptable, flexible, agile organizations. The manager's importance to the reengineering process is to remind the organization that radical process innovation should consider marketplace perspectives and not just the internal perspectives of senior-level management and the company.

Reengineering causes dramatic process improvements that are too often only demonstrated in individual process areas, not in sales revenue results. Managers should play a key role in companywide reengineering. In addition to giving employees and salespeople convincing reasons for a new design and the ability to provide feedback in the form of concerns and suggestions, management must also look outside the organization to the customers for direction.[5] The drive to win more business from those ever-smarter customers has spurred a wave of change in the sales profession. Many leading companies are completely overhauling the way they hire, organize, train, and compensate their sales forces. Their aim is to turn their salespeople into smart *businesspeople.*

Managers generally view reengineering as change that occurs quickly and dramatically and involves the radical redesign of cross-functional business processes. A study of reengineering projects at forty companies during the past three years observed several instances in which senior executives slowed down the pace of change and modified ambitious reengineering goals. Although these companies did not gain the breakthrough improvements often promised by proponents of radical reengineering, they nonetheless reduced the cost of specific processes by 30 to 50 percent, shortened cycle times, and dramatically improved service to their customers.[6]

To stay ahead of the competition some companies are hiring representatives who are industry experts, not mere glad-handing extroverts. They are also organizing their sales forces around customer industries and national accounts, not just geographic territories. In addition, companies train salespeople to probe customers' business problems, not peddle products and manipulate buyers. They are compensating salespeople for building long-term partnerships with customers, not for driving short-term revenues. Sales forces are expected to deal with complex issues and problems, and they are expected to come in and size up the situation. Reengineering the organization around customers and channels is one of the major ways sales forces are starting to achieve significant revenue gains and cost reductions.[7]

Effective marketing relies on a two-way information flow between the marketer and the prospect. Marketers must collect detailed demographic and lifestyle information about large numbers of consumers to determine effective market segments. Then they must integrate this mass of information into a concrete understanding of what products different consumers want and what they are willing to pay.[8] Fundamental reengineering means adopting a new marketing approach. The most common one observed is mass customization. Rather than mass-market a standard service to all customers, mass customization produces and delivers individualized services to each customer and at costs competitive with mass production.

VALUE FOCUS

Firms are focusing on what adds value for the customer and eliminating what does not. This means that firms have to ask, "Is what we're doing useful enough for someone to pay money for it?" Although value means different things to different people, it consists of intrinsic product features, service, and price, but price is not everything in determining value (see Figure 3.1). For example, a study by Grey Advertising determined that only 37 percent of its customers currently compared prices, contrasted with 54 percent in 1991.[9]

With deregulation and a growing global economy, service marketers now face the pressures experienced by product companies a decade ago. The new value concept offers individualized benefits rather than more standardized offerings. Thus, the strategy of producing more of

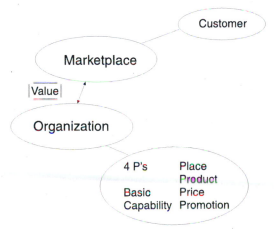

FIGURE 3.1. Importance of Understanding How Customers Define Value

the same service is replaced by innovation and differentiation based on mass customization. Since sophisticated services such as finance or insurance are knowledge based and information intensive, the marketing goal is to reengineer them to integrate knowledge and information in a way that is different and better than the competition. Reengineering is about business reinvention—not business improvement, business enhancement, or business modification. Reengineering should be done only when a need exists for a major overhaul.

A business insurance seller reengineered its organization so that agents could do complete policy illustrations and ready-to-sign contracts in the field with customers. Previously, headquarters staff controlled the data necessary to complete a policy and were perceived by agents as unnecessary middlemen who slowed or sometimes killed the sale. The new approach is agent focused, not only by giving each agent a personal computer, but also by transferring systems and data-processing staff into the field closer to the point of sale. Agents can tap the necessary data from across the corporation, perform needs analysis instantly as the customer looks on, and illustrate various insurance programs to satisfy specific customer requirements. The internal support structure that makes this possible is invisible to customers, who view the buying process as seamless and not entangled in insurance company bureaucracy.

Evidence suggests that corporate reengineering may trigger the outsourcing of an internal activity to an external supplier. The objective is to free up company technology, systems, and staff for more strategic activities. For example, Eastman Kodak turned over the management and maintenance of its telecommunications system to Digital Equipment Corporation so it could concentrate on imaging technology. Xerox Corporation also outsourced many computing activities as part of its back-office reengineering. The resulting services contract with Electronic Data Systems (EDS), estimated at $4 billion, makes it one of the largest outsourcing deals in history.

VALUE-ADDED FEATURES

A *process* is a collection of activities that takes one or more kinds of input and creates an output that is of value to the customer. Service marketers are reengineering customer engagement approaches to find opportunities that create new market segments rather than share existing ones with competition. Reengineering projects have been initiated to search for prospects in areas never before considered and have proven to be an effective way to cut costs and reduce payrolls. However, reengineering gets just as much impact from increasing sales as it does from decreasing costs, either by taking market shares from competitors or generating new products and services.[10]

The value-added feature is not in the product anymore; it is in the relationship between the company and its customers. In an economy with euphemistic concepts such as downsizing and reengineering, there has to be added value in giving customers the help companies no longer have in house. If customers perceive a high level of expertise in the company and believe it can help them, then the company is worth more to them.[11]

Too many managers feel the only time they need to restructure their departments or sales force is after something major has happened, such as losing a big account. Many do not think ahead and realize that a realignment may be able to help problems that have not even come up yet. The best companies first focus on which customers they want to serve and then learn what those customers need and how they can fulfill those needs.

Studies show that 80 percent of the companies in the United States have imbalanced alignments. They have too many salespeople in one territory and too few in another, thereby costing companies 2 to 7 percent in sales losses every year. Realignment is not a static concept that happens only once during the life cycle of a company. Usually, it is an evolutionary process that is implemented in various stages to meet new customer or industry demands. Competitive firms are always aware of the chance for change; they are the ones that are always surveying their customers and sales representatives to find out what they want. They are also keeping a keen eye on the competition and staying aware of the changing nature of their marketplace. Then, they are acting upon these changes and needs through a combination of crisis management and reengineering efforts (see Figure 3.2).

The only way American companies can survive today is by moving from an internally based product focus to a more external customer focus. Sales forces that take the time to understand their customers and learn what they want are the ones that will succeed. The most important thing is understanding and meeting the needs of the customer.[12]

FIGURE 3.2. Customer dialogue through CABs can help develop effective strategic systems to respond to volatile market conditions.

CUSTOMER SATISFACTION

Hundreds of Fortune 500 companies and many small and midsize companies have some sort of customer satisfaction initiative under way. Companies such as Dow Chemical, Eastman Chemical, IBM, Ralston Purina, 3M, and Xerox are surveying customers and collecting data on satisfaction levels to identify and resolve obstacles for better customer relations, to formulate sales and marketing strategies, and to retool sales and service skills.

Too often, customer satisfaction initiatives fail or provide misleading results because they ask the wrong questions of the wrong people and produce data that are used in the wrong way. The problem is compounded when a company fails to inform the customers it has surveyed about how their input has changed the way the company does business. On the other hand, companies that have successfully used customer surveys have learned key lessons: how customer satisfaction is measured can often be as important as what is measured, and having an adaptable surveying methodology ensures that listening to the voice of the customer reflects market forces.

For example, Xerox uses phone surveys and goes after decision makers exclusively, conducting about 10,000 surveys per month. It has also gone beyond measuring customer satisfaction to gauging customer loyalty as well. Xerox continues to measure satisfaction but also asks whether the customer would recommend Xerox to an associate and whether he or she would buy from Xerox again. The company also tracks survey data by three classes of customer—first-time buyers, replacement or upgrade buyers, and additional buyers—giving the company a finer read on who purchases what, when, and why. Xerox has also implemented a Customer Relationship Assessment survey for its top customers. The goal, again, is to go beyond satisfaction to look at customer loyalty. These are face-to-face surveys conducted by the account management teams of about 500 global, national, or "named" accounts that are essentially Xerox's best customers.[13]

Businesses have been trying to become more profitable by re-engineering and downsizing. Winning more business from existing customers is critical to meeting its objective. IBM underwent a major sales force reorganization when Louis Gerstner took over as chairman. A major reason why Big Blue was floundering at the time was that salespeople had lost touch with customers and had failed to spot new revenue opportunities. Droves of sellers representing multiple fiefdoms of IBM—hardware, software, consulting services—would call on a client, creating confusion. Many customers, particularly major ones, wanted a single face that represented IBM's vast array of products and services. Consequently, one of Gerstner's first moves was to implement a system in which a single client executive would work with accounts and manage teams of product representatives, systems engineers, and consultants within IBM. These client executives have become, in effect, experts in the customers' industries.

The term *partnering* gets bandied about in business circles. For companies that are building lasting relationships with clients, the concept is simple—partnering means becoming part of the customer's business fabric. Partnering also means continually finding ways to provide more value to customers by jointly developing new products to help them improve their business processes. The goal is to become so enmeshed with customers that they naturally come to that particular firm for solutions, and the salespeople become virtual employees of the customers' company. Being a consultant with customers often means educating them about the full range of a company's products.[14]

CUSTOMER ORIENTATION

Customer orientation is making the greatest inroads in the business world. In a recent Forum Corporation survey, more than 600 executives were asked, "What are your organization's most important strategic needs?" Of the respondents, 86 percent answered "quality of customer service." Unfortunately, although many organizations make a serious effort to find out what their customers want, they do not effectively use this potentially powerful data.

By failing to follow up, these companies deny themselves a great opportunity. Today, being customer focused is not enough. When management incorporates the voice of the customer into the company, and then acts on it, the organization is transformed. It goes from being merely customer focused to being customer driven. In the era of the customer, the companies that succeed will be the ones who reshape the "interesting" data from their customer research and implement them in imaginative and powerful ways.[15]

As communication tools become interactive, managers talk more about goals that pertain to individual relationships, such as share of customer requirements, customer contact outcomes, and customer satisfaction measures. Managers have begun to think of good marketing as good conversation and as a process of drawing potential customers into progressively more satisfying back-and-forth relationships with the company. American Airlines' use of the frequent flier program in 1981 triggered other industries to create membership clubs. Retention programs, if skillfully designed, can be much more than volume discount programs; they can inspire loyalty from the market's biggest spenders. The key is to deliver benefits that appeal more to heavy users than to light users, draw attention to a brand's claimed distinction, and enliven the buying experience so that the heavy user becomes an even heavier user.[16]

For example, resellers of long distance telephone service have gained market share at the expense of the major carriers in the United States, while in Europe travel agents undercut the airlines by buying blocks of seats from whoever has the lowest rates at any given time and then reselling them. However, interconnection also allows competitors to become a source of customers for one another when one provider originates traffic and another eventually delivers it.

NETWORKS

Network-based businesses are those which deliver a significant portion of their value to their customers by transporting people, goods, or information from any entry point on a network to any exit point. These businesses can be categorized by the degree to which their value to customers resides in the network or in the individual outlets.[17]

Most industries are struggling under worldwide overcapacity; steadily improving productivity maintains this glut even as companies shut down plants. The Atlanta-based unit of Siemens that makes heavy electrical equipment and motors has halved floor space since 1986, yet is producing 50 percent more. Buyers are in just the mood to push such companies to the wall.[18]

Ninety percent of accounts leave a particular company because they feel badly treated and unappreciated. That should serve as a warning signal to companies to make sure their perception of customer satisfaction matches the reality. Implementing a process to repair its damaged accounts by identifying the problems, meeting with the customer and assessing the damage, and focusing time and attention on fixing the situation are part of the recovery.

Management should devise a realistic strategy to repair the client relationship. Once a reconciliation with a customer is reached, companies should notify everyone involved. "Organized learning must take place, not just in marketing and sales departments, but company wide. Share the story with everyone in the organization so it does not happen again."[19] Customer focus should always be a top priority during, and after, any reengineering effort.

CASE STUDY: SALES STRATEGY, IBM SOFTWARE GROUP

Synopsis

Cross-selling complementary products to existing customers could be a source of growth for IBM's Software Group.

Background

IBM's Software Group (SWG) is a $13 billion business for IBM, representing about 15 percent of IBM's revenue and over one-third of its profits. The software industry is comprised of application software, operating systems software, and "middleware" software, which is where IBM's SWG focuses its efforts. The middleware market is further segmented into four categories of software products: (1) database, (2) application server, (3) systems management, and (4) e-mail and collaboration. Correspondingly, the SWG consists of

1. DB2 for database systems,
2. WebSphere for Web application servers,
3. Tivoli for systems management, and
4. Lotus for e-mail and collaboration.

These product divisions compete primarily with Oracle, BEA systems, Computer Associates, and Microsoft, respectively.

IBM SWG has expanded its sales force from a few hundred when it was formed in 1995 to close to 8,500 today. About 10 percent of the salespeople are software product generalists and are charged with the following tasks: developing and maintaining relationships at key accounts with customers and the other IBM hardware and services salespeople at their accounts; identifying product-specific opportunities and passing on the leads to the appropriate product specialists; and closing large complex deals. Around 70 percent of the sales force are product specialists who are tasked with identifying customers' needs.

Problem Headline

Cross selling of IBM's software is the focus.

Description

While about 80 percent of IBM SWG's sales is repeat business from existing customers, only about 20 percent of IBM SWG's revenue results from the sales of new middleware products to existing customers. Our two closest competitors obtain about 40 percent of their revenue from the sale of new products to their existing customers. Although IBM's software business is currently enjoying better-than-industry-average growth rates, leveraging existing customer relationships to sell complementary products could be a new source of potentially significant growth.

If well over 80 percent of customer implementations involve at least two and quite often three or four categories of middleware, what is keeping the SWG from cross selling today? Why has the bulk of SWG's sales force been trained, incented, and motivated to focus exclusively on selling one of our four product lines, i.e., "operate with blinders on" and disregard opportunities for other IBM products?

The four product divisions within the SWG are very autonomous and each funds its own sales organization. Two of the divisions are the results of acquisitions, and each is headed by very strong product general managers.

To further complicate matters, the salespeople are also highly autonomous, work from mobile offices, and do not get the opportunity to develop relationships with their peers in the other product divisions. Furthermore, the organization almost unanimously shares some common beliefs. First, the sale of middleware is highly technical and requires a high degree of specialization. If an SWG sales rep for one product line introduces a product from another product line in the sales process, this will complicate the sale, delay the time it will take to close the deal, and invite further competition.

Say, for example, that a sales rep for the WebSphere product line is working with a prospect that is looking to extend an existing application onto the Internet to allow its customers to see their account balances. In addition to considering IBM software, this prospect is also considering a solution from BEA Systems and expects to complete the product evaluation and purchase the middleware in one month. It is also very likely, though, that this prospect in the near future will require a new database and the Oracle salesperson. Plus, the IBM WebSphere salesperson has decreased his or her odds of winning the deal because now the customer is very likely to consider Oracle's application server product.

Alternate Solutions

Early in 2001, the product specialists were given training in identifying opportunities for products in other SWG product lines, and they were offered a significant "cross selling" bonus on top of their commissions for selling solutions involving products from multiple SWG product lines. These actions have had minimal impact on the sales reps' behavior.

Question

What suggestions do you have concerning how a CAB or reengineering can help address this dilemma?

Chapter 4

Customer Alliance and Trust Building in Relationship Formation

Relationship marketing has moved rapidly to the forefront of academic marketing research and practice. It even sometimes is referred to as a new paradigm for theory and practice. Recent explorations have begun to provide some insight into consumers' valued relationships with businesses and with brands. Related research explores the use of preexisting social ties to stimulate economic exchanges.

The services marketing literature has explored customer–service provider relationships more thoroughly than other research streams in marketing because of the unique characteristics of both relationships and services. Some research distinguishes service relationships that are functionally (or constraint) motivated from those which are socially (or dedication) motivated, the latter being more relational in character. Other services research suggests that certain service encounters are liable to be more similar to a meeting between friends than merely economic transactions. Research on service encounters indicates that reciprocal self-disclosure, an important factor in friendship formation, can contribute positively to commercial exchange satisfaction. Finally, without unpacking the meaning of the term *friend,* other researchers identify some consumers who think of retailers or service providers as friends.

The absence of conceptual clarity about what relationships, especially friendships, mean in marketing contexts is inimical to the successful deployment of relationship marketing. In popular use in North America, the term *relationship* has become so hackneyed and carries so many meanings that it may have little connotative force in marketing. Indeed, many customers may find the idea of commercial relationships oxymoronic, manipulative, undesirable, or incredible. Charging ahead with relational programs without an understanding of what marketing relationships can and cannot be puts the cart before the horse.

THE NATURE OF RELATIONSHIPS

Explorations of relationships in North American social science find that relationships involve a longer time period than a single encounter and each interaction episode is influenced by other interactions. Two people are in a relationship with each other if they have impact on each other, if they are "interdependent" in the sense that a change in one person causes a change in the other, and vice versa. The more specific term *friendship* is portrayed as a voluntary, personal relationship, typically providing intimacy and assistance, in which the two parties like each other and seek each other's company.[1]

Relationship research specializes in particular relationships, notably dating, marital, and mother-child relations, but not commercial relationships. A review of the friendship literature provides some indications of what we may find in commercial friendships. Yet, the friendship literature does not address specifically the incidence, nature of, or contexts for commercial friendships. Nevertheless, in North America, at least some people mobilize their notions of friendship in managing repeated commercial exchanges. We find examples of businesses, ranging from jewelry stores to restaurants, life insurance companies to brokerage houses, banking services to automobile brands, that promise clients friendship in their marketing communications. Thus, the use of friendship as an idiom for commercial relationships is worth exploring, although there is a paucity of specific hypotheses for an analysis of friendships formed in commercial contexts. Frequently mentioned features of friendship include intimacy, loyalty, honesty, trust, and enjoyment of each other's company.

In general, friendship is depicted as expressive rather than instrumental. In other words, friendships are not generated or sustained for extrinsic material benefits that accrue. Perceiving that one party is sustaining a friendship for instrumental purposes is likely to damage it. Nevertheless, friendships originate in settings in which cooperation and friendly relations serve instrumental goals. People also use friends to achieve a variety of objectives and, in this sense, serve instrumental ends. In short, instrumentality is a key tension framing many adult relationships and is particularly evident in work relationships.[2]

Regular and frequent interaction is an important correlate of friendship formation and maintenance. In fact, sociability is viewed by most as intrinsic to friendship. Nevertheless, time may be spent socializing with people who are not regarded as friends, and "true friends" may not socialize very often. Complexities relating to the relationship between sociability and friendship contribute to the ambiguity surrounding the construct. Thus, we expect that frequent and regular interactions, combined with outcome dependency, are likely to promote "friendly relations" that may be viewed as superficial acquaintanceship by one party and as a stage in the formation of a friendship by another.

Friendships vary along a continuum from agentic to communal. Agentic relationships are based on joint activities and projects, characterized by fairly explicit individual rights and "tit for tat" reciprocity, limited in emotional investment, and maintained for as long as their benefits to self exceed their costs. Communal relationships are based on wide-ranging conversation and joint activities, characterized by diffuse mutual responsibilities and obligations, or generalized reciprocity. They are deepened by emotional attachment and empathy and maintained through shared commitment and personal loyalty.

Structural, individual, situational, and dyadic factors must coalesce for friendships to form. Friendships first require structural opportunities for sociability. In other words, proximity affects the formation of friendships. Other research details how shared environments influence the formation of friendships. If an environment presents structural opportunities for interaction, persons then may look for rejection factors, such as disliked characteristics. That is, they first decide whom they do not want as friends. The unsuitability of a candidate for friendship involves drawing inferences about overlap in personality, norms, or lifestyles. Judgments about unsuitability have received little empirical investigation.[3]

Finally, individual persons, situations, and dyadic interaction patterns together determine whether a potential friend actually will become one. Research has focused on individual characteristics, such as attractiveness, social skills, responsiveness, and similarity, that contribute to the formation of friendships. Much less studied are situational characteristics. Research suggests that anticipating future interactions, frequent interaction, outcome dependency, and availability for friendship greatly enhance the likelihood a friendship will develop. Marketers will note that these situational factors characterize many exchanges in services, channels, and industrial relationships. However, situational nuances in exchange contexts may inhibit commercial friendship formation.

The rising popularity of marketing has forced many companies to adopt the relational approach rather than the transactional approach when dealing with their exchange partners. Against this backdrop, trust has been repeatedly identified as the key ingredient for building successful relationships.

According to Johanson and Nynes, the older a relationship, the greater the likelihood it has been through a critical "shakeout" period of conflict occurrences by both exchange parties.[4] If the dyad survives this period, the foundation is created for personal trust and a good working relationship. Furthermore, members of the dyad become better acquainted with each other, which enables them to predict each other's reactions. Therefore, we hypothesize the following:

1. There is a positive association between the length of time the buyer has known the seller and the buyer's trust in the seller.
2. There is a positive association between the length of time the seller has known the buyer and the seller's trust in the buyer.

ROLE OF TRUST

Trust, which has been conceived as a confidence in the reliability and integrity of an exchange partner[5] and a willingness to rely on that confidence,[6] is thought to be a building block or foundation for satisfactory interactions. This definition suggests that trust leads to satisfaction in the exchange relationship between buyers and sellers. Rournier and Mick regard trust, along with satisfaction, as a component of relationship quality.[7] They find that relationship quality significantly influences the customer's anticipation of further interaction with the salesperson. Anticipation of future interaction is considered a desired outcome of relational exchanges or dyadic encounters. It reflects the nature of the intended relationship the buyer has with the seller[8] and includes dimensions such as whether the buyer intends to discuss and continue to conduct business with the seller. The best predictor of a customer's likelihood of seeking future contact with a salesperson is the quality of the relationship to date, which reiterates the significance of a satisfactory working relationship between the exchange parties. Hartline, Maxham, and McKee indicate that trust increases the likelihood that buyers will anticipate doing business with the supplier firm in the future.[9] Holden finds that when buyers have high levels of trust in a salesperson and company, they are more likely to pursue more cooperative negotiations and open communications, which leads to a more productive relationship.[10] The positive consequences of trust are acknowledged by Martin, who finds that trust in the salesperson leads to a desire to interact with that particular salesperson again.[11] Given the interrelationship among trust, satisfaction, and anticipation of future interaction, the following can be hypothesized: *the buyer's trust in the seller is positively related to the buyer's satisfaction with the seller.*

IMPORTANCE OF LISTENING

Interpersonal communication between salesperson and customer has been widely discussed as an important part of successful sales interactions. More specifically, an important aspect of the communication process is the ability to listen effectively. A survey of industrial purchasing agents suggested that, from the customer's point of view, listening may be the single most important skill that salespeople can possess. Conversely, a study of industrial salespeople found that one of the most important reasons that salespeople are unsuccessful is failure to listen. Although several conceptual models of salesperson-customer communication and interaction have been developed, none of these models has included listening as an independent component. True listening is different from hearing. Hearing is passive; it happens. Listening, on the other hand, involves not only our ears but our eyes, heart, and gut; it leads to understanding.

Understanding refers to an individual's ability to accurately ascribe meaning to incoming messages, both verbal and nonverbal, and includes the emotion behind the words (e.g., thoughts and feelings) as well as their literal meaning. *Interpreting* incoming information involves comprehending its implications. Salespeople relate new incoming information to preexisting knowledge about similar and dissimilar sales situations. *Evaluating* refers to the assessment of the appropriateness of the information and the process of placing value on the messages. Salespeople's primary task when evaluating is to prioritize information so that they can concentrate on the key concerns. *Remembering* involves updating material in memory. The processing flow is cyclical, since material in memory dictates the way incoming information is understood, interpreted, and evaluated.[12]

When face-to-face with a person, effective listening goes beyond the words being said to the physical expression of communication—body language, for example. It is important to become an empathetic listener, asking follow-up questions, restating what has been said, making it clear that you are listening, and using body language, such as leaning forward, smiling, nodding your head, and maintaining eye contact. The whole point of empathetic listening is not just that you "get" what the other person is saying, but that the other person knows you got it.[13]

Salespeople every day miss important facts, nuances, desires, and needs of clients because they simply don't listen. Most people do not like to be sold to; they like to buy. If someone is talking, then they are not getting the opportunity to buy. Most people forget that good listening also requires a high respect for silence. Become more comfortable with silence. It allows for breathing room, especially in a sales situation. It encourages prospects to talk, and they may tell you something really critical. The importance of listening can hardly be exaggerated.

SUCCESSFUL LEADERSHIP AND EMOTIONAL INTELLIGENCE

Today's workforce requires a different kind of leader than ten years ago; leaders who can inspire people and lead teams are essential in organizations. Leadership is becoming more focused on the psychological needs of human beings. The old dictator-type leadership style no longer works as well. Motivation and inspiration energize people, not by pushing them in the right direction, but by satisfying some basic human needs for achievement, a sense of belonging, self-esteem, and recognition. When workers believe that their managers care about them, they are more likely to perform better, and the financial results support this.

Good leaders motivate people by articulating the organization's vision in a way that stresses values to the audience they are addressing. True leadership deals with ideas about what to do, providing a sense of vision and optimism.[14] This makes the work important to the individuals performing the task. Leaders also involve people in deciding how to achieve the organization's vision, which gives people a sense of control. Another important element is providing coaching, feedback, and role modeling, thereby helping people grow professionally and enhancing their self-esteem. Finally, good leaders recognize and reward success, which not only gives people a sense of accomplishment but makes them feel that they belong to an organization which cares about them.[15]

Every businessperson knows a story about a highly intelligent, highly skilled executive who was promoted into a leadership position only to fail at the job. Every businessperson also knows a story about someone with solid, but no extraordinary, intellectual abilities and technical skills who was promoted into a similar position and then soared.[16] Such anecdotes support the notion that having the "right stuff" is more art than science.

Professional excellence stems from more than just technical skills and intelligence quotient (IQ); emotional intelligence has come to play a pivotal role in differentiating extraordinary leaders from the rest (see Box 4.1). Leaders with a high level of emotional intelligence not only are successful but also know how to create a culture that is characterized by greater morale, increased employee satisfaction and productivity, improved return on investment in change efforts, and great success at achieving organizational goals.[17]

Dr. Daniel Goleman, CEO of Emotional Intelligence Services and affiliate of the Hay Group, wrote an international bestseller, *Emotional Intelligence,* and the recent business bestseller, *Working with Emotional Intelligence.* For twelve years, Dr. Goleman reported on behavioral sciences for *The New York Times.* Daniel Goleman presents a compelling business case for assessing and developing emotional intelligence in employees. According to Goleman, emotional intelligence is the "street smarts" in people, reflecting on their ability to deal successfully with other people, their feelings, and the everyday social environment. By dealing with these pressures successfully, they positively influence their overall well-being.

BOX 4.1. Emotional Intelligence

Cultural Intelligence in Negotiation

Dealing with manager and executives from different cultures
Accommodating your cultural counterparts
- Language
- Dietary considerations
- Behavioral habits

Emotional Intelligence in Management Decisions

Forward-looking decisions that focus on opportunities rather than
    problems
Forging new directions into the future instead of fortifying old ones
Identifying new levels of excellence
Keeping friendship separate from the decision-making process—
    objective and fair

Successful leaders have always been attuned to human interaction, and their decisions imbued with emotional sensitivity. According to Goleman, leaders need high emotional intelligence because they represent the organization to the public, they interact with the highest number of people within and outside the organization, and they set the tone for employee morale. In addition, leaders with empathy are able to understand their employees' needs and provide them with constructive feedback.[18]

The term *emotional quotient* (EQ) was developed by Dr. Reuven Bar-On in 1985 to describe his approach to assessing aspects of general intelligence. Bar-On, a clinical psychologist currently directing emotional intelligence research at the University of Haifa in Israel, has been researching the area of emotional and social intelligence since 1980. Bar-On's research is cross-cultural, describing and assessing the emotional, personal, and social components of intelligent behavior. Bar-On defines emotional intelligence as "[a set of] capabilities, competencies, and skills that influences one's ability to succeed in coping with environmental demands and pressures, and directly affect one's overall psychological well being." Bar-On's theory of emotional intelligence (EI) is the most comprehensive theory on emotional and social intelligence, and growing research has suggested that EQ is a better predictor of "success" than the traditional measures of cognitive intelligence (IQ) (see Box 4.2).

The IQ test measures an individual's native intelligence. The test has been used for decades and has been proven reliable; that is, it gives reliable constant readings on any one person over time. Arguably, a high IQ has been found to be correlated with success in college and more loosely associated with good jobs, health, and long life. EQ is meaningless from a scientific perspective; that is, there is no adequately researched EQ test, and anyone claiming to be able to give you a number that represents your EQ is perpetuating a hoax.[19] Nevertheless, EQ tests are increasingly given by employers to screen potential candidates, yet no one can legitimately claim the test yields an EQ figure similar to an IQ test result.[20] The first comprehensive and scientific measure of emotional performance was the BarOn Emotional Quotient Inventory (EQ-i), which measures one's overall EQ. The test examines five composite factors—intrapersonal and interpersonal skills, adaptability, stress management, and general mood—along with with fifteen other subcomponents of EQ designed to quantify one's ability to cope with the daily demands of life (see Box 4.3).

Recent research has shown that EQ may be more important than one's IQ. EQ can also be called *character quotient,* because it purportedly measures the qualities of character. Studies state that people with high EQ seem to fare better in life, are more well adjusted, and more successful in their careers. In fact, says Goleman, an individual's success at work is 80 percent dependent on EQ and only 20 percent dependent on IQ. The Carnegie Foundation for the Advancement of Teaching uncovered a similar fact, revealing that, in such

---

BOX 4.2. Measures of Intelligence

IQ—Intelligence Quotient

- Measures a person's native intelligence
- Proven scientifically reliable

EQ—Emotional Quotient

- Measures components of a person's values and character
- Scientifically meaningless

BOX 4.3. Components of Emotional Intelligence

- *Self-awareness*
  The ability to recognize and understand your moods, emotions, and drives, as well as their effect on others
- *Sale-regulation*
  The ability to control and redirect disruptive impulses and moods
- *Motivation*
  A passion to work for reasons that go beyond money or status
- *Empathy*
  The ability to understand the emotional makeup of other people
- *Social skills*
  Proficiency in managing relationships and building networks

---

technical lines as engineering, about 15 percent of one's financial success is due to technical knowledge and about 85 percent is due to skill in human engineering—attributed to personality and the ability to lead people (see Box 4.4).[21]

According to leadership expert Warren Bennis:

> In those fields I have studied, emotional intelligence is much more powerful than IQ in determining who would emerge as a leader. IQ is a threshold competence. You need it, and it does not make you a star. Emotional Intelligence can.

A groundbreaking study of information technology professionals discovered that different segments of the technology community have different levels and kinds of emotional intelligence.[22] Multi-Health Systems, Inc. (MHS), a leading test publishing company recently tested the emotional intelligence of 104 information technology (IT) specialists using the BarOn EQ-i. With the average score of 97.5, IT personnel were found to have lower EQ than other groups, such as human resources professionals, who were also tested and had an average score of 110. The highest scores were among the technical support staff and the lowest among the programmers. It was traditionally believed that technical specialists with high IQs were the best performers. However, it is the IT technical specialists with the high EQ who use their interpersonal skills to access more information and get help solving problems, and they are generally better liked by

BOX 4.4. Leadership Styles and Emotional Intelligence

Coercive—Drive to achieve, initiative, self-control

- Demands immediate compliance—"Do what I tell you."
- Works best in crisis, to kick-start a turnaround or a problem employee
- Negative impact on work environment

Authoritative—Self-confidence, empathy, change catalyst

- Mobilizes people toward a vision—"Come with me."
- Works best when clear direction is needed
- Mostly positive impact on work environment

Affiliative—Empathy, building relationships, communication

- Creates harmony and builds emotional bonds—"People come first."
- Works best when motivation is needed during stressful circumstances
- Positive impact on work environment

Democratic—Collaboration, team leadership, communication

- Forges consensus through participation—"What do you think?"
- Works best when seeking buy-in or consensus
- Positive impact on work environment

Pacesetting—Conscientiousness, drive to achieve, initiative

- Sets high standards for performance—"Do as I do, now!"
- Works best when seeking quick results from highly motivated and competent teams
- Negative impact on work environment

Coaching—Developing others, empathy, self-awareness

- Develops people for the future—"Try this."
- Works best when wanting to help an employee improve performance
- Positive impact on work environment

others. A survey of 150 IT executives of the nation's 1,000 largest companies conducted by RHI Consulting found that 68 percent of IT executives felt that "soft skills" were more important now than they were even five years ago.[23]

The ability to confront and address difficult human interactions, particular professional accountability issues, requires highly emotionally intelligent individuals. In other words, it requires people who have an awareness and understanding of their own feelings and the feelings of others they manage (see Box 4.5). The late David McClelland, a Harvard University psychologist, found that leaders with strengths in a critical mass of four or more EI competencies were far more effective than peers who lacked such strengths. His research analyzed the performance of division heads at a food and beverage company and found that, of the leaders with this critical mass of competence, 87 percent were in the top third for annual salary bonuses based on their business performance. In addition, their divisions on

---

BOX 4.5. Using Emotional Intelligence

In Delegation

- Clearly communicate information up front:
    Clarifies objectives and provides direction.
    Diminishes fear and uncertainty.
    Gives staff a sense of the importance of the assignment and enhances their self-esteem.
- Ensure that staff are sufficiently familiar with the overall details—know specific strengths and weaknesses.
- Maintain and encourage open communication with those under your direction.

In Negotiation

- Tell the truth, the whole truth, and nothing but the truth in explaining your position at the outset.
- In your presentation, include how you feel about the situation.
- Avoid emotional issues that are tangential to the issue at hand—"stick to the facts."
- Try to appreciate what the other party wants to get out of this negotiation.

average outperformed yearly revenue targets by 15 to 20 percent. The managers who lacked EI were rarely ranked as outstanding performers. In fact, many of them underperformed by an average of almost 20 percent.[24]

CASE STUDY:
CONSUMER SALES, CAMPBELL, INC.

Synopsis

Production and distribution inefficiencies as well as the inability to meet customer demands are the primary problems confronting us at this time.

Background

Campbell, Inc., is a 160-year-old manufacturer of power equipment. The sales force consists of forty salespeople, five of which represent national accounts, one being the nation's largest home improvement retailer.

Problem Headline

Production and planning decisions override forecasting plans from sales personnel. Distribution turnover is increasing; lead time and fill rates are decreasing. Campbell needs to develop strategy, by account, for production on a rolling twelve-month plan.

Description

Managing the nation's largest home improvement retailer has posed two significant problems.

First Issue: Production

The growth from this national account has been exponential over the past eight years. Because of this, many manufacturers in the industry are aligning themselves to accommodate demand. However, our company has not. EMT philosophy regarding inventory over the years has been to work lean, keeping restocking levels throughout the country extremely low. When the customer experiences a surge of sell through for any given reason, demand exceeds supply.

The number one rule for this customer is "Ship 100 percent complete and on time!"

Second Issue: Distribution

Congruent with the first issue, the ability to ship to this customer complete and on time has been a continual struggle. We believe this is partly due to the wages EMT is willing to pay for pickers, forklift operators, and loaders. In addition, lead time for import products fluctuates dramatically, especially with specific Asian suppliers. With the production issues outlined earlier, it becomes nearly impossible to react to customer demands with such extreme lead times.

Alternate Solutions

Production

A recent recommendation was that the company increase inventory levels on the 20 percent of items that drive 80 percent of the business. This would give us the opportunity to react when needed on key items while keeping in mind the company's philosophy regarding inventory.

Question

How can Campbell, Inc., use a customer advisory board to accelerate a reaction and hear a definite decision?

APPENDIX: SENIOR-LEVEL MANAGEMENT AND CUSTOMER ALLIANCE BUILDING

Utilize the most senior corporate executives in the corporation in sales and marketing support of national/global account managers (N/GAMs) responsible for relationship management of key and strategic accounts.

Objectives

- How to make an executive partnership program effective in your company
- How to develop the key drivers that make these programs work
- Overview benchmarking findings
- Understand program details of a specific company
- Provide a practical view of field implementation

Key Elements

- Developing an executive champion
- Defining the role of the senior executive

- Defining the roles of the NAM/GAM
- Account/executive assignment process
- Senior executive contact training
- Results measurement
- Operational support
- Recognition

Benchmark Findings

- Compaq—Executive Sponsor Program (ESP)
- Xerox—Focus Executive Program (FEP)
- IBM—Partnership Executive Program (PEP)
- Hewlett-Packard—Assigned Executive Program (AEP)
- Ardmore Group—Assigned Corporate Executive (ACE)
- Lucent Technologies—Customer Alliance Program (CAP)

How long has your program been in existence? Eight to twenty-nine years

Which organization manages the strategy? Sales or customer satisfaction department

How many executives participate in the strategy? Depending on how the accounts are stratified within each company, from twenty-plus to over 100

How are accounts selected for the program? Strategy value and revenue contribution

Which level of executives participates in the strategy? CEO and all senior executives—at a minimum

How are executives selected to participate? Volunteer, matching process with account team input

How many accounts does each executive cover? Two to six per executive

How many calls are executives expected to make annually? Two to six per year

How long does the executive remain in the assignment? For his or her entire career

What is the role of senior-level management? Establish executive relations, door opener, customer satisfaction, customer advocacy, consultant to account team, resolve difficult issues quickly

How are executives measured? Annual surveys, self-assessment

Do the executives receive any incentives? No bonuses or cash rewards, but award systems in place

Is training offered to the participating executives? On occasion—how to make an executive call!

Is there strong support for the strategy? Supported by every CEO in benchmarked companies

How important is the strategy? An absolute requirement for key account strategic coverage

Role of Senior-Level Management

- Establish shared value and strategy with customer executive.
- Develop relationships with senior customer executives.
- Open closed doors.
- Capture and communicate words of the executive customer.
- Champion the resolution of executive customer issues.
- Assist NAM/GAM in account strategy.
- Participate as team member.
- Schedule four customer calls per year.
- Host all event marketing programs.

Objectives of Senior-Level Management

- Ensure major account customer base considers you the "vendor of choice" through executive interaction.
- Understand customer business drivers.
- Increase the level and breadth of executive relationships.
- Communicate your company strategy.

Roles and Responsibilities of Senior-Level Management

- Assist in development of account strategy—minimum one time/year.
- Meet with customer executives—as agreed, usually two to four times/year.
- Host quality events, product announcements, etc.—as agreed, usually one to two times/year.
- Identify key business, work processes of executive customer—one key process identified, documented, and responded to/year.
- Champion the resolution of executive customer issues—as required.
- Establish ongoing relationship with NAM/GAM.

Roles and Responsibilities—NAM

- Ensure all accounts have an appropriate executive partner (EP)—ongoing.
- Develop the account strategy—minimum one time/year: communicate and agree on strategic account plan with executive partner; conduct internal account reviews and facilitate executive involvement.

- Manage the partnership with the executive—as agreed: agree and document specific expectations and activities planned; share your objectives with your executive; manage communications with the executive; facilitate executive involvement in the account.
- Jointly with EP, identify key business and work processes of the executive customer and map solutions to the process—one key process identified, documented, and responded to/year.
- Promote customer utilization of the EP program—ongoing.
- Provide staff support to the executive (call briefing materials and logistics, general follow-up)—as required.
- Utilize EP program processes—ongoing.

Program Office Responsibilities

- Account assignment process
- Performance reporting and results measurement
- Operational support
- Executive customer issue/opportunity communication
- Recognition

Performance Measurement

- Account revenue growth
- Successful identification of major new business opportunities
- Account input demonstrating understanding of company's strategy
- Effective capture and communication of "the voice of the customer"
- Level and quality of relationships developed
- Satisfaction level of the NAM/GAM[25]

SECTION II:
BUILDING CUSTOMER ADVISORY BOARDS

Chapter 5

CAB Structure, Procedures, and Agenda

Companies often have difficulty when they try to launch a novel product or service by imagining what the customer's response is going to be when they come in contact with the product or service that is being offered. Some firms choose not to ask the customer's advice, they do not watch what the customer does, nor do they try to comprehend what the customer wants. Mostly they function on the basis of calculated assumptions.

The key to success is not in hypothesizing, but in being knowledgeable, comprehending and giving your client what he or she desires. One of the most effective strategies to do this is to form a CAB. CABs most commonly include nine to twelve different customers from your target sector who act as "mystery shoppers" to tap into customers' attitudes and beliefs. This provides insight into what will continue the customers' business.[1]

The more frequently CAB meetings are held, the more successful a business will be. Some businesses hold weekly CABs and others have monthly or annual forums (for some specific computer companies' CABs, see Box 5.1). If the same board members meet with one another each time, then meetings should be held less often—about three to four times a year. Most effective CABs meet for two to three hours, while some meet for a full day. Most of the time, customers who attend a CAB are rewarded for their contribution. Some of the types of rewards are gift certificates (from a retailer), free weekends away (from a hotel group), lunch or dinner (from a restaurant), a free service (from a motor dealer), a free pair of prescription designer sunglasses (from an optician), etc.

CABs are instrumental in discovering what the customer wants, which is a two-step process. The first step is to discover what the customer actually wants, and the second, to deliver *plus* more. Deciding

---

BOX 5.1. Computer Industry Customer Advisory Boards

Hewlett-Packard/Customer Advisory Council

- Has under twenty members
- Meets once a year
- Uses suggestions for R&D

Sun/Customer Advisory Board

- Has twelve members
- Meets once a year
- Purpose is to advise Sun's directions on key issues

Microsoft/Global Executive Roundtable

- Has fifty members
- Meets twice a year
- Focus is on business development of top global accounts

Digital Equipment/Customer Advisory Board

- Has sixty members
- Meets twice a year
- Members play an advisory role in Digital's policy setting

---

what the customer wants is a vision step. This is how a business can create a vision or a picture of customer service excellence. It is advisable that a business first begin with the end result of the business in mind; the vision must be specific and it needs to be written down. "Delivering plus more" is a principle that entails the concept to underpromise and overdeliver. This is an excellent principle for businesses to abide by so as not to make too many promises to the customer. Most times businesses make promises that they cannot keep. Underpromising businesses are able to overdeliver, surprising their customers with complimentary incentives. Often this type of business practice will lead to a flow of continuing business.

FORMING A CAB

Many firms shy away from advisory boards because they seem like an administrative nightmare. Companies that use them successfully often get around that problem by enlisting their local partners to manage them.[2]

Step One: Set Objectives

Research shows that customer boards take many different forms. The first step is to work out a clear "mission statement" for these meetings. Options to consider include the following:

- Market intelligence
- Industry news and trends
- Product evaluation
- Finding new applications and markets

Start Small

If you are concerned that these meetings will take too much time or be outside a budget, start small and informally and organize a lunch with major buyers whenever you visit the target market. In markets where prestige matters, such as Latin America, create wall plaques identifying customers as members of the CAB. Ideally, the number should be around ten to twenty board members who also match your markets demographic as closely as possible. This way, they'll cast a critical eye on your business practices while still giving you insight into a buyer's decision-making process.[3]

It's important to remember that a board can be far more effective than standard market research because board members are empowered to offer proactive advice that can affect the company instead of just offering a snapshot of the market. Besides members' business acumen and matching the market demographic, this group provides the company with guidance on difficult decisions, so they should all to a certain degree embody the core values and standards that the company seeks to embody.

Step Two: Decide Whom to Invite

The board helps develop products and services that meet customer needs and gives local buyers a chance to network with others in their industry. Here are three groups to consider when selecting board members:

1. *Existing customers:* You can select a cross section or target a subgroup to increase visibility, for example, zero in on industry opinion leaders. To solidify major accounts, you might want a board of key customers, or if you want to increase penetration of an underserved segment, you may want a panel of these customers.
2. *Potential buyers:* Targeting potential buyers, even if they currently buy from another supplier, can be a sure route to getting intelligence about competitors.
3. *Former buyers:* Research shows that 40 percent of buyers who defect do not say why they are leaving; nearly 90 percent will never return to their original supplier. So finding out why companies are leaving, and preventing them from going, can make a difference.

The quality of a board's contribution depends on the quality of its members. When board members are well informed and take their membership seriously, the company is more likely to get information that impacts the bottom line. Make diversity a priority—different perspectives help a company approach its business from new and varied angles—in such areas as demographic segment, geographic location, revenue potential or reputation in the industry or marketplace. Each board member is likely to be curious about the qualifications of the others and will want to feel that he or she is in good company. Also, the caliber of the people selected may challenge the more competitive members to make a contribution that is as good as or better than everyone else's.[4]

As part of board maintenance and improvement strategy, decide how long each member should serve. For as long as your board's members provide useful ideas or information, you may want to stick with your winning team. On the other hand, to be sure a board and company do not stagnate, it may prefer to limit board members' tenure to a year or two. Regularly assess the changing needs and circumstances of a company and board members and go with the flow. Keep in mind that the board members retained should have demonstrated the ability to learn and interact with other board members and company employees, to ask focused questions, and to provide relevant and informed feedback on company policies, procedures, and performance. Whatever board members' rate of turnover, have them meet at last twice a year to be sure they make a positive impact.[5]

Benefit of CABs

Companies concerned about privacy issues may prefer to take advice from customers rather than let outsiders view their inner workings. Choosing board members with care may develop an advisory board with authorities in several different fields, who can provide expertise on a wide range of business issues. Also, customers want to know that the companies they buy from care about them, and forming an advisory board shows that a company values customers' opinions and wants to improve products and service methods. Offer a board membership to thank a loyal customer or even to lure a new one. Board members may benefit personally and professionally from networking with one another. Although market research may be costly and unreliable, CABs are extremely cost-effective and may provide more useful and accurate information.[6]

BOARD COMPOSITION AND PROCEDURES

Customer advisory boards should be made up of ten to twenty members. Ideally, members should be senior-level managers with decision-making authority in their own organizations. It is also advised to target as board members people with knowledge in areas where the company is weak (see Box 5.2). For example, a company might try to draft a technology expert for help with finding opportunities on the Internet.

To avoid any appearance of impropriety, board members should not receive financial compensation. Many managers are willing to serve on a CAB for the opportunity to impact another company's business policy in a way that benefits their own companies or simply for the prestige.[7]

Once a board has been formed, it should meet two to four times per year. If the CAB uses different customer groupings each time, every three to four months would be appropriate, but meetings involving

BOX 5.2. Customer Advisory Board Members and Roles

- *Executive owner, Al Koeppe*
  Empower customer council
  Provide leadership and direction
  Lead the customer vision and mission
  Champion the customer initiative
- *Executive sponsors*
  Accountability at all levels
  Lead by example
  Drive the customer initiative
  Develop and communicate vision
- *Customer council*
  Internalize customer and inclusion into the company culture
  Set annual customer objectives and measure deliverables
  Provides council updates through steering committee to executive
  sponsors and owner

Joe Ward	External Affairs
Shirley Jones	Business and Operations Manager
Rosa Wormley	External Affairs
Sheila Schmidt	HR Business Partner
Peter Pullins	HR Business Partner
Sally LaRocca	HR Business Partner
Ray Nadler	Transmission
Jeff LaRossa	Distribution
Kathy Martelo	Distribution
Jeff DiNardi	Distribution
Joe Clayton	Appliance Service Business
Steve Ellis	Media Issues
Charles Goncalves-Rooney	Customer Ops.
Isabel Sharkey	Customer Ops
Charles Forline	Delivery Operations Support
Tia Miller	Corporate Rate Counsel

- *Steering committee*
  Integrate customer plan into business strategy and goals
  Align HR policies and practices with customer plan
  Support customer structures

Joe Ward	External Affairs
Shirley Jones	Business and Operations
Rosa Wormley	External Affairs
Sheila Schmidt	HR Business Partner
Peter Pullins	HR Business Partner
Sally LaRocca	HR Business Partner
Steve Ellis	Media Issues
Ray Nadler	Transmission

- *Consultants*

Peggy Smith	Human Resources
Jill Pomerantz	Law Labor and Employment
Ellen Moore	Dev. and Org. Effect
Joe Branca	Staffing
Susan Flynn	Commodity/Supplier Management

the same board members could be held less frequently. The most effective CABs meet for two to three hours. Agendas could include company strategy, production, marketing problems, and customer satisfaction, service, development, and education/communication. Most of the information given to the board will already be in the public domain. There's usually no need for hard-core proprietary data, but companies should lay out the ground rules with prospective board members at the invitation stage so they will know before they join what is expected of them in terms of confidentiality. If a CAB is going to discuss issues involving private information, members should be asked to sign a confidentiality agreement.[8]

TYPES OF CABs

Three types of CABs tend to be found in use in software companies. The first is associated with overall corporate strategy, the second with product planning and project selection, and the third with detailed planning and evaluation of new product/version plans. They differ in terms of size, makeup, frequency of meetings, and, of course, objectives. Variations of these types deal with specific market or geographic segmentation of customers, such as a telecommunications advisory board or a German market advisory board.

Corporate Strategy Boards

Corporate strategy boards are populated with executives from customers who represent markets in which you have future interest. They are usually current customers, though not necessarily. Members need to be of a high enough executive level to allow exploration of a broad range of topics and should possess a degree of future vision that makes the conversation valuable to the vendor—and to other members of the board. Dialogue on corporate strategy boards is about vision and future value and is often not restricted to product issues alone. Some commonly considered questions are as follows:

- Where should we be heading to better serve your needs?
- How do you view the competitive landscape of our industry?

- How do you see the industry changing in the next few years and what will drive those changes?
- What are the attributes of a future successful vendor in this market space?
- How can we improve the return on your investment in our products and services and the ease of doing business with us?
- What future product offerings would be valuable to you and how would it improve our competitive position?

Product-Planning Boards

Product-planning boards are usually made up entirely of current customers who represent a broad view of needs for the next set of product releases. Members are managers or lead implementers who have specific knowledge about how your products are used and where the real user opportunities lie. Discussions on these types of boards are led by product management and R&D managers and center around the following questions:

- Where is our product underperforming for you?
- How exactly do you use our product? How might that change in the future?
- What are your requirements and how do they compare and contrast with those of other members of the board?
- How would you rate various packages of enhancements?
- How would you apportion our R&D budget among new products/modules, current product extensions and enhancements, platforms and porting, and maintenance/bug fixing?
- What is the competition saying about us? How do they position us? Do you agree?
- Here is a sneak preview of the next version—can you "beat us up" early to help us improve it?

Launch Success Boards

Launch success boards have been used successfully by many software companies to incorporate continuously the voice of the customer into the process of specifying and evaluating an upcoming new product or version release. Members of such a board are typically advanced users of the product who are knowledgeable about usage patterns and needs at their sites. While planning and strategy boards will meet between one and four times per year for one to two days, time commitments for launch success boards are often much greater. One Midwest software vendor invited five diverse customers onto such a board and asked for a commitment of one-fourth of their time for a year to improve the content, quality, and market impact of a major rearchitecture of its product line. Board members spent one week a month at the vendor site to communicate requirements and to describe usage scenarios to requirements engineers, designers, and lead developers. As early prototypes became available, they logged hours operating them and provided feedback and guidance. These board members eventually formed the core of the beta-testing programs for later versions and served as early reference sites for marketing and public relations campaigns.[9]

Much of the work of launch success boards is done one-on-one with development personnel; however, early sessions are held with the entire "cross customer" group together, to facilitate learning from one another and jointly setting priorities.

CABS AND NEW BUSINESSES

A CAB can give an emerging company a jump start by providing access to expertise and experience from a wide range of necessary disciplines: finance, marketing, product development, and personnel, to name a few. Moreover, advisory board members do not have the legal liability they would assume as officers or directors. In many cases, advisory board members are predisposed to getting involved without compensation. After all, they may appreciate getting in on the ground floor of an enterprise and understand that they could gain an opportunity to invest in the project.

Inventors can identify a problem and create a solution. They must realize, however, that an idea becomes a business through an engine composed of many different components—talented individuals and a fuel called money. The casual observer may be surprised to learn that many entrepreneurs—people full of fresh, fertile ideas—have very little business experience. These innovators often get advice to help navigate the perils of starting what hopefully will become an international concern. Part of the exercise should be selecting an advisory board. Entrepreneurs will most certainly turn to professional services firms, lawyers, and accountants to sort through a maze of intellectual property, finance, tax, corporate, and securities issues.

An advisory board, as opposed to a corporate board, is a selected group of volunteers who are knowledgeable about technology, interested in entrepreneurial endeavors, and willing to spend time with the principals of a project. They are frequently part of the business, professional, or academic communities. This group of people can validate an opportunity and dramatically accelerate the entrepreneur's learning curve. They can network with people who have the resources to make that technological dream a business reality. They eventually may even become players in the business. Advisory board members often can entice other people to come on board before committing money, as well as identify financial goals for short-, intermediate-, and long-term needs. These strategic connections make for good personal chemistry and increase the odds of getting funds crucial to meeting business goals.[10]

Lawyers, accountants, venture capitalists, and recruiters are frequently candidates for an advisory board because they are bound by a code of confidentiality, and they are generally well connected. They have direct and indirect relations with good thinkers and workers, even though they are judicious in how they use their contacts. They also have to be trusted as an integral part of the team to ensure open lines of communication. Over time, that trust must be nurtured, developed, and managed.[11]

It is common practice for a start-up to form advisory boards that bring technical, marketing, and other advice—as well as prestige—to the company (see Figure 5.1). The advisers often work for companies that later become business partners with the startup. One issue that arises is whether these advisory boards are simply a means to funnel stock grants to outsiders in an effort to win their business. Some companies seek to avoid this through company policies regarding CABs. For example, some organizations have a conflict-of-interest policy; an employee can no longer accept remuneration for serving as an adviser or director for any customer or potential customer.

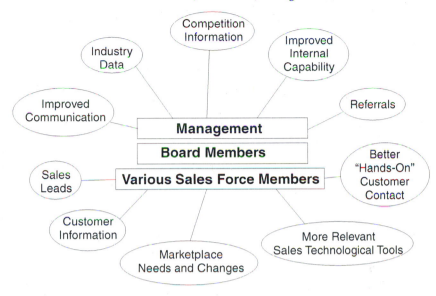

FIGURE 5.1. Customer Advisory Board Structure and Potential Benefits

CASE STUDY:
SALES MANAGEMENT AND MEASUREMENT, EMEA

Synopsis

Our sales structure and measurement is entirely locally focused. More and more customers are requiring a global quote and delivery of products and services on a global basis. A new sales measurement structure is needed to handle effectively major international deals.

Background

We provide computer systems (servers, storage, PCs, and services) to worldwide customers. Each country's subsidiary has identified key local distributors that handle most of the product sales and shipments. In addition, each subsidiary has sales, marketing, warranty, and services operations locally.

Our customer (Company X) is a multinational corporation operating in twenty countries in Europe and in additional locations around the world.

They run data centers—large centers where computer systems are housed and managed.

Problem Headline

We need to develop sales management, measurement, and compensation plans to handle key multinational accounts.

Description

Company X wants to purchase all of its computing products from us through central purchasing in one location (United Kingdom) and have them shipped directly to their subsidiaries worldwide. Once the products arrive in each country, Company X needs local service to install and provide warranty on those products as well as local sales attention and support. In some instances, there are also cooperative marketing agreements in place that also need to be "rolled out" by local sales and marketing organizations.

Under current measurement systems, our country manager, the sales team, and the services team do not get recognition for this sale as it was purchased entirely in the United Kingdom. Needless to say, their interest in "helping" is low. Customer satisfaction is at risk.

In addition, most of our product shipment and fulfillment is handled via distributors in every location. One of the distributors in France recently met with our management, complaining that he recently lost business with the Company X account because purchasing and delivery would now be handled centrally in the United Kingdom. He told us that this was jeopardizing our long-standing relationship and he was considering carrying another line of products to compensate for the lost business.

Today in Company A

Sales management and measurement is all locally based. Countries are run as separate profit and loss (P&L) operations with country managers measured on their overall PandL performance versus goals. Goals for the sales teams reflect this local structure. Retirement of quote results only when revenue is received in the country PandL.

Question

How could a customer advisory board help in this situation?

APPENDIX: SAMPLE CAB AGENDA

Landmark Hotel in London, England
April 7-9, 2004
Theme: Building for the Future

Monday, April 7, 2004

08:00-12:00	Check-in and Welcome Package Pickup
12:30-13:30	Lunch
13:30-15:00	Customer Case Studies
	Dave Butler, Director, Global Information Systems, Dow Chemical Company
	Fred Bystrand, Vice President, Group Information Systems, AAB
15:00-15:30	Afternoon Break
15:30-17:30	Customer Roundtable
	Allen Feryus, Senior Vice President, Information Services, New York Mercantile Exchange
19:00	Welcome Reception

Tuesday, April 8, 2004

07:00-08:00	Breakfast
08:00-08:30	Welcome, Introductions, and Overview of Agenda
	Nancy Stevens, Vice President and Customer Programs
	Allen Feryus, Senior Vice President, Information Services, New York Mercantile Exchange
08:30-09:30	Corporate Strategy and State of the Company Discussion
	Bob Smith, Chairman of the Board, President and CEO
09:30-10:00	Morning Break
10:00-10:30	PCBU Update and Strategy
	Bruce Rodgers, Vice President and General Manager, Worldwide Sales and Marketing
10:30-11:00	Service Capabilities
	John Randle, Vice President and General Manager, Services Division
11:00-12:00	Breakout Session 1 for Concurrent Workshops A, B, and C (each session will be given three times)
	A. Making Enterprise a Reality—A Microsoft Exchange Case Study
	Lucy Quinn, Vice President of Strategic Marketing and Brand Management

Kannakote Srikanth, Vice President and General
Manager, Network and Systems Integration
Services
B. Managing the Environment
Tim Leisman, Vice President and General Manager,
Operations Management Services Business Unit
Nigel Bufton, Strategic Development and Marketing
C. Global Pricing—Indirect Fulfillment Option
Tom Vacchiano, Vice President, WW Business
Operations and Planning

12:00-13:00	Lunch
13:00-13:30	Customer Meeting
13:30-14:30	Breakout Session 2 for Concurrent Workshops A, B, and C
14:30-15:00	Afternoon Break
15:00-16:00	Breakout Session 3 for Concurrent Workshops A, B, and C
16:00-17:00	Alliances Update
	Robert Bismuth, Vice President, Corporate Strategic Alliances
17:00-17:45	Customer Meeting
19:30	Gala Dinner

Wednesday, April 9, 2004

07:00-08:00	Breakfast
08:00-08:30	Customer Feedback from Day 2 and Review of Action Items
	Allen Feryus, Senior Vice President, Information Services, New York Mercantile Exchange
08:30-09:00	Financial Outlook and Discussion
	Alexis Makris, Vice President and Controller, Business Operations
09:00-10:00	Panel Discussion: CAB Members Question
	Allen Feryus, Senior Vice President, Information Services, New York Mercantile Exchange
	Executives: Bob Smith, Chairman of the Board, President, and CEO
	Bruce Rodgers, Vice President and General Manager, Worldwide Sales and Marketing
	Harry Cooper, Vice President and General Manager, Products Division
	John Randle, Vice President and General Manager, Services Division

	Bill Saunders, Vice President, Corporate Strategy and Technology Group and Chief Technical Officer
10:00-10:30	Morning Break
10:30-11:15	Panel Discussion: Questions for CAB Members
	Bruce Rodgers, Vice President and General Manager, Worldwide Sales and Marketing
11:15-12:00	Corporate Strategy Development Dialogue with CAB
	Bill Saunders, Vice President, Corporate Strategy and Technology Group, and Chief Technical Officer
12:00-13:00	Lunch
13:00-14:00	Year 2004 Program Discussion
	Sam Fuller, Vice President and Chief Scientist
14:00-15:00	Customer Loyalty/Ease of Doing Business Discussion
	Dick Fisher, Vice President and Chief Information Officer
15:00-15:30	Afternoon Break
15:30-16:00	CAB Organization Discussion and Next Steps
	Allen Feryus, Senior Vice President, Information Services, New York Mercantile Exchange
16:00-16:30	Review of Action Items and Close
	Bruce Rodgers, Vice President and General Manager, Worldwide Sales and Marketing

Attendee List

ABBA Asea Brown Boveri Ltd.
ASZ Automatiserng Sociale Zakerheid BV
AUDI AG
Bank of America
Banque Paribas
Barclays Bank PLC
British Gas PLC
Canadian Federal Government
Carrier Corporation
Ciba Specialty Chemicals
The Dow Chemical Company
DuPont Information System
GAK Groep
GEC/General Electric Company PLC
LEGO Systems A/S
MATIF S.A.
New York Mercantile Exhange
Philip Morris U.S.A.

Reuters Limited
Robert Bosch GmbH
Sharp Corporation
Shell International Limited
SmithKline Beecham Pharmaceuticals
SNCF
Swiss Federal Government
Tele Danmark EDB
Union Bank of Switzerland
UTC/Pratt & Whitney
VW of America Inc.
The World Bank

Chapter 6

Value of CABs to Customers and Organizations

In recent years, customer satisfaction research, initiated by the widespread adoption of the marketing concept, has been significant. Efforts to align marketing strategy with the goal of maximizing customer satisfaction have been pursued in earnest by product and service providers. Data show that postpurchase research, "largely including customer satisfaction work," accounted for one-third of revenues received by the largest U.S. research firms. Subsequent data confirm the trend, showing that the number of firms that commissioned satisfaction studies increased by 19 and 25 percent in the United States and Europe, respectively.

Evidence from Bain & Company suggests that, of customers claiming to be satisfied or very satisfied, between 65 and 85 percent will defect. Moreover, in the automobile industry, in which 85 to 95 percent of customers report that they are satisfied, only 30 to 40 percent return to the previous make or model. A shift in emphasis from satisfaction to loyalty appears to be a worthwhile change in strategy for most firms because businesses understand the profit impact of having a loyal customer base, as demonstrated by the figures provided by the associates of Bain & Company. These data report that the net present value increase of 60 percent in profit results from a 5 percent increase in customer retention. Moreover, others have noted that the relative costs of customer retention are substantially less than those of acquisition.[1]

With these exceptional returns to loyalty and the concomitant emphasis firms should devote to loyalty programs, why are defection rates among satisfied customers as high as 90 percent? The answers to these questions rely heavily on a greater understanding of the role of customer satisfaction in loyalty, other nonsatisfaction determinants of customer loyalty, and their interrelationships. It is necessary to begin the determined study of loyalty with the same fervor that researchers have devoted to a better understanding of customer satisfaction.

CUSTOMER SATISFACTION AND LOYALTY

The many definitions of both satisfaction and loyalty describe what consumers do to become satisfied and/or loyal. For example, satisfaction has been defined as an "evaluation of the perceived discrepancy between prior expectations . . . and the actual performance of the product." Generally, loyalty has been, and continues to be, defined in some circles as repeat purchasing frequency or relative volume of same-brand purchasing. Of note is the definition of loyal customers as those who rebought a brand, considered only that brand, and did no brand-related information seeking. All these definitions suffer from the problem that they record what the consumer does.[2]

Satisfaction, defined as pleasurable fulfillment, is when the consumer senses that consumption fulfills some need, desire, goal, or so forth. Thus, satisfaction is the consumer's sense that consumption provides outcomes against a standard of pleasure versus displeasure. For satisfaction to affect loyalty, frequent or cumulative satisfaction is required, so that individual satisfaction episodes become aggregated or blended. As will be argued here, however, more than this is needed for determined loyalty to occur. The consumer may require movement to a different conceptual plane, in all likelihood, one that transcends satisfaction.

In accord with this distinction, loyalty has been defined quite differently. In a modification of the definition, to include the act of consuming, loyalty is described here as a deeply held commitment to rebuy or repatronize a preferred product/service consistently in the future, thereby causing repetitive same-brand or same-brand-set purchasing, despite situational influences and marketing efforts having the potential to cause switching behavior.[3]

Over the past decade, many companies have become skilled at the art of customer relationship management. Few companies have bothered to look carefully at the broad context in which customers select, buy, and use products and services. As a result, companies have routinely missed chances to expand sales and deepen loyalty. Customer advisory boards allow a company to listen and keep in touch with their customers, a very effective way to build trust and promote retention. Boards will obviously never replace talking to customers during sales calls, but they do provide a formal interface where the buyer-seller relationship is based on honesty, not negotiation (see Box 6.1).

GAINING THE "COMPETITIVE EDGE"

Research shows that many of the marketing coups of recent years have been far from customer centric, or, at least, the successes have proceeded from a deeper understanding of what people want than would ever emerge from the bowels of a data mine. Whatever people may desire of their products and services, they adamantly do not want kowtowing from the companies that market to them.[4]

What do customers want? There are dozens, if not hundreds, of research tools available to probe the answer to that question—for a price. New research conducted strongly suggests that companies with industrial customers should employ a little-used tool that will supplement their market research without emptying their coffers: the CAB. CABs—groups made up of senior executives from companies that are current or prospective customers—are a powerful way to monitor customer satisfaction. These boards are underutilized, even though they are a practical, available, and dynamic way for companies to stay in touch with their most important asset.[5]

A 1996 study, "Customer Advisory Boards As a Sales Tool for the Customer-Relationship-Building Process," found that of the seventy Fortune 500 companies surveyed, twenty-one had CABs, and, of those companies, nineteen found such groups to be an extremely or

---

BOX 6.1. Value in Customer Advisory Boards

- Customer loyalty
- Feedback on strategy, technology, and products
- Business development potential
- One-on-one interaction with senior executives from top customers
- Advisory role
- Promotes relationship building

somewhat effective tool in the customer relationship–building process. According to this research, one of the main benefits of a CAB is that it provides a continuing dialogue with current and potential customers instead of the static information of market research, providing companies with the competitive advantage of ongoing involvement with their customers. That many other companies do not have CABs is also a competitive advantage in itself. One food-production company included in the study found that its customer base was eroding. When its executives turned to the CAB for help, the board gave them suggestions on how to track defections and how to develop and implement a system that provided continuous customer feedback. As a result, the company was able not only to stem the flow of customer defections but also to reverse the trend, rebuilding its customer base.[6]

New research shows that only one in four firms uses a customer board. Those which do use them, however, rave about the results. CABs build loyalty with key customers and set companies apart from the competition. The research found that these boards increased sales, built strong buyer loyalty, strengthened foreign partnerships, and provided valuable market intelligence.

Advisory boards help companies understand what is foremost on their customers' minds; thus, they can be a vehicle for developing new prospects. When managers who are not yet customers are invited and respected for their involvement and suggestions, it makes it easier for them to consider becoming customers.

Whereas customer surveys let buyers contribute to success, advisory boards actually recruit buyers to play for your team. In many ways, advisory boards ask customers to cross over from being customers to being associates and advocates of a company. The benefits of a CAB add more value than ever to buyers' transactions and add more buyers than ever to a database.[7]

CASE STUDY:
SALES MANAGEMENT, NORTH AMERICAN OPERATIONS,
TIA ELECTRONICS, INC.

Synopsis

Tia Electronics needs to develop a method to drive the Sales Management System as a guiding set of principles to plan and execute short-term and long-term revenue and profit objectives for new and incumbent sales managers. This involves creating a training solution to teach these principles to new sales managers throughout North America.

Background

Tia Electronics (TE) is the world's largest distributor of electronic components and computer products, with 2000 sales of $13 billion. Our global distribution network spans the world's three dominant electronic markets—North America, Europe, and the Asia-Pacific region. TE serves as a supply channel partner for more than 650 suppliers and 200,000 original equipment manufacturers (OEMs) and commercial customers through more than 225 sales facilities and twenty distribution centers in thirty-nine countries.

The North American Components Division consists of eight operating companies, which are segmented by customer need:

- TE/Bell Components specializes in servicing the needs of small, medium, and emerging industrial OEMs.
- TE Contract Manufacturing Services (CMS) Distribution Group focuses exclusively on providing distribution services to contract manufacturers.
- TE/Richey Electronics specializes in serving the passive, electromechanical, and connector needs of North American original equipment manufacturers.
- TE Semiconductor Group specializes in serving the semiconductor needs of North American OEMs.
- TE/Wyle Communications specializes in serving the semiconductor needs of communications and networking OEMs regardless of size.
- TE/Zeus Electronics specializes in serving the needs of military, aerospace, and high-reliability electronics manufacturers.
- Marubun/TE is a joint venture, wholly owned by Marubun Corporation and Tia Electronics, Inc. Marubun/Arrow is a customer-focused business, supporting customer needs, with design work and vendor selection often done in Japan and production taking place in Asia or North America.
- TE Vision is specifically aimed at providing technical-engineering solutions to manufacturers of advanced radio frequency, microwave, and fiber-optic components.

Problem Headline

Drive the NAC Sales Management System as a guiding set of principles for new and incumbent managers.

Description

The president of TE's North American Components Division wants to institutionalize a common set of sales management practices and processes to ensure enduring top- and bottom-line growth across TE's business groups. In 1998, the NAC president, who is now CEO, asked our department to partner with field managers and Alexander Group, Inc., to develop TE's NAC Sales Management System.

Individually, the different sales management practices and processes can be viewed as "pillars" that support TE's growth objectives. Together, these pillars form an integrated Sales Management System. While every sales manager will have unique opportunities and needs, the core practices and processes within the system remain consistent across all business groups.

Since 2001, TE has held six NAC sales management conferences to communicate this information to our sales management team. There were approximately 350 managers at the first conference; this number grew to close to 600 managers at the last one, held in February 2000. The Training, Management, and Organization Development Groups led design teams of field managers to gather best practices and to develop new tools and system resources to make our goal of enduring profitable growth a reality. Our data indicate that there is a correlation between using the practices and principles from the Sales Management System and performance to plan. Specific measurements are in place for each pillar, and managers are held accountable for them in the branch plan and in their own performance evaluation.

The Sales Management System has been delivered two or three modules at a time at the NAC sales management meetings. Anyone who was appointed to a management position after February 2000 has not received formal training to learn the entire system. In addition, if a manager was appointed anytime after the first conference in March 1998, he or she may not have been exposed to all of the modules. Every NAC manager has a large binder that contains reference material for each module. This year, we distributed the most current data on CD-ROM. We rely on managers in the field to teach the newer managers.

The Sales Management System is the common set of practices and principles, but each business group has unique applications of it depending on the customers being served. For example, the process of planning is very similar, but the thresholds, targets, and key drivers could be different depending on the business group.

Part of our growth strategy also includes a focus on mergers and acquisitions. Since the first conference in 1998, we have had a major integration each year in North America, with several other smaller acquisitions. We have conducted compressed training sessions for newly hired general managers who have come on board due to an acquisition.

The Sales Management System was designed to give managers a road map to plan and execute short- and long-term revenue and profit objectives.

Our sales offices are scattered throughout the United States, and they serve a diverse group of customers. As the number of TE employees continues to grow, we run the risk of the message becoming diluted. The bottom line is that we need to find a way to provide just-in-time training to newly hired sales managers and to enable incumbent managers to remain focused on and disciplined in using the practices and principles.

Alternate Solutions

The conferences were the main vehicle used to communicate the information. Although these conferences were also used as team-building events, they began to become less effective as the years progressed. Due to the mergers and strategy refinements, we had to repeat certain topics a few times, which was frustrating to more experienced managers. The pace was often too fast for newer managers, which caused many of them to become confused.

A team is in the process of designing and developing a sales leadership course for new managers. The design called for a Web-based component, but this was cut due to budgetary constraints. The Web-based solution would have provided self-paced instruction whereby new managers could learn the basics before attending a course, as well as allowing incumbent managers to brush up on skills.

Question

What role could a customer advisory board play in developing the Sales Management System as a guiding set of principles for new and incumbent managers?

SECTION III:
STRATEGIC USES
AND EFFECTIVE MANAGEMENT

Chapter 7

Customer Satisfaction at Prudential Insurance

Recently, Prudential Insurance Company of America found itself at the most critical point of its 121-year existence. In an industry that relies upon trust, it was facing a large, highly publicized scandal that seriously called into question the ethics and values of the company. In addition, the company's financial future was not at all promising, as customers defected due to a stagnant product line and the company's reliance on an outdated business model. Prudential had always been a leader in the insurance industry and was known for many innovations. It lost this innovative edge, however, and only offered to customers the products it wanted to sell, rather than those that customers wanted to buy. During the past few years, the financial services landscape was undergoing change at an ever-increasing pace, as customer needs radically changed the marketplace.

Information became more accessible, and customers became smarter and began to gain more control in the company-customer relationship. It became clear that insurance companies were no longer essential for customers to meet their most important financial needs. Instead, customers faced unprecedented choices in the management of their finances. New products were made available and new ways for customers to access them were created.

ORGANIZATIONAL CULTURE

Prudential was desperately in need of a culture change. A company's culture consists of its beliefs, values, structures, and policies. In his text *Marketing Management*, Philip Kotler notes that "changing corporate culture is the key to implementing a new strategy successfully."[1] To effect this culture change, Prudential developed a customer-centric core vision and strategy that would align the efforts of the entire company. The Prudential vision became "to be a leader among financial services companies in the delivery of insurance and investments to individuals and institutions both domestically and abroad," and their strategy, "to provide customers with the advice and information they seek, the distribution options of their choice, and the products they demand, supported by excellent service."[2]

To be successful, this strategy would need to be executed with a focus on both customer needs and financial priorities. Prudential then began a campaign to increase the business literacy of all employees and to help them realize the impact their actions have on a customer. This campaign required that each of the company's 60,000 employees take a day out of their daily functions for a full day of interactive learning. Each employee now understands the changes occurring in the financial services industry, how the company earns and spends its money, what customers expect and want, and what Prudential must do to win in the marketplace. Kotler notes that "visionary companies set ambitious goals, communicate them to their employees, and embrace a high purpose beyond making money." The first steps taken by Prudential, which compare favorably to this list, helped to successfully change the culture of the company.[3]

CUSTOMER ACQUISITIONS

Acquiring customers in today's marketplace is an extremely difficult task. Customers are smarter and more demanding than ever before, and the competition for their loyalty is intense. Companies are continuously trying new strategies that will facilitate the identification and acquisition of profitable customers. Many current strategies involve developing a stronger, deeper relationship with a company's existing customers, the thought being that relationships entail some degree of loyalty, last longer, and ultimately increase the value of the customer base. One such strategy is referred to as one-to-one marketing. In the article "Is Your Company Ready for One-to-One Marketing?" Rogers describes a relationship in which the customer tells the company of a need and the company customizes its products and services to meet it. Over time, the interaction and continuous modification becomes convenient for the customer and makes leaving for a competitor less appealing.[4]

Prudential's Customer Acquisition and Program Management Unit

The implementation of such a program requires an infrastructure that enables the differentiation of customers. This facilitates identifying a company's most valuable customers, so that their needs could be met first. Among the benefits of one-to-one marketing are increased cross selling, reduced customer attrition, and higher levels of customer satisfaction. At Prudential, a Customer Acquisition and Program Management Unit was created and is currently piloting a one-to-one marketing program. The unit utilizes a centralized customer database that cuts across business groups to identify Prudential's most valuable and profitable customers. It exploits opportunities for cross selling to increase the number of products owned per customer and per household. It also manages numerous programs related to the generation and distribution of high-quality leads. One such program uses wireless technology to transmit leads to agents in the field.[5]

In addition to one-to-one marketing, another strategy to acquire customers involves the targeting of minority groups. Many minority groups are growing at extraordinary rates and are quickly becoming target markets in many industries. Procter & Gamble, for example, has been exploring ways to reach the Hispanic population more effectively. Similarly, an article in *Fortune* titled "Smart, Minority-Friendly Television" describes the tremendous success that HBO and Showtime have experienced targeting minority-based markets.[6]

At Prudential, the Customer Acquisition and Program Management Unit conducted a comprehensive market needs study to understand the U.S. ethnic market picture. It is currently seeking to improve the company's penetration into the Chinese, Korean, Hispanic, and African-American consumer markets by launching lead generation campaigns, creating new marketing materials, and getting involved in community action initiatives.[7]

CUSTOMER RETENTION

Although acquiring new customers is critical to any business, it is much more critical for a company to retain the customers it has. To do so, a company must consistently exceed the expectations of its customers and maintain their high satisfaction levels; provide quality products at a good price and support the products with excellent service; implement a system that allows customers to complain easily and the company to resolve complaints quickly; and focus on gaining the loyalty of its customers, as loyal customers have the most value. Acquiring new customers is much more expensive than retaining current ones. By the same token, increasing the customer retention rate can be enormously profitable for a company.

For instance, 93.6 percent of Prudential's existing policyholders renewed their policies. Increasing this rate to 95 percent, an increase of only 1.4 percent, would increase renewal premium revenue by $74 million each year. As it is more costly to acquire new customers than to retain existing ones, many companies have established formal customer relationship–building programs. This is necessary because 91 percent of unhappy customers will never again buy from a company that dissatisfied them and they will communicate their displeasure to other people. Prudential has numerous programs, such as the one-to-one marketing pilot program, that focus on customer relationship building with the goal of satisfying and retaining customers.[8]

In addition, Prudential Insurance implemented a campaign that targets customers who start to express an interest in surrendering or transferring their insurance policies. To date, this program has been successful and defection rates have decreased. The company has also implemented a companywide process to manage better the relationship the company has with new customers. Other programs that have been implemented utilize direct marketing to increase persistency and cross selling and win-back campaigns that target the lost customer base.

INITIATIVES TO IMPROVE CUSTOMER SATISFACTION

The key to retaining profitable customers lies in the satisfaction they obtain from doing business with the company. The more satisfied a customer is, the stronger the bond between customer and company will be, and the greater the loyalty the customer will have toward the company. Today, companies must strive to offer products that provide customers with excellent value, and they must do so in a way the customers prefer and that exceeds their expectations. Customers expect to get the products they want, when they want, where they want, and how they want, i.e., delivered in a pleasingly professional manner at a reasonable price (see Figure 7.1 and Table 7.1).[9]

Voice of the Customer Unit

For many years, Prudential saw its customer base erode, as dissatisfied customers left the company in droves. Prudential formed the Voice of the Customer Unit. This unit reached out to Prudential's lost customers to obtain feedback and identify the reasons they left. The most frequent complaints dealt with Prudential's written communication with its customers. Specifically, complaints referenced statements and bills that were incomprehensible, multiple statements if a customer owned more than one product rather than a consolidated

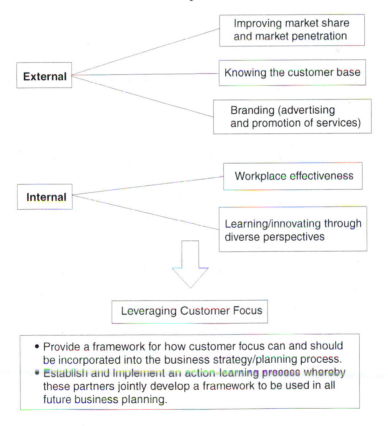

FIGURE 7.1. Strategic Customer Focus Building Blocks

TABLE 7.1. Strategic Customer Focus

Expected Outcomes	Process
Increased capacity of both human resources and business strategists/planners to use and apply a "leveraging customer focus lens" in all aspects of their planning process	Meetings with key stakeholders • Identify key strategic initiatives • Review current database and needs
An overall PSEG and business operations information base that assists in developing competitive advantage and business effectiveness as it relates to diversity (market segments, etc.)	Kick-off session for strategic partners Four action-learning capsules focusing on customer and marketplace potential Information gathering and organization with partners throughout the process Development of a communication and information-sharing mechanism for sustaining a leveraging perspective

statement that contained everything, and even that insurance correspondence was cold and heartless at a time when families were grieving over the death of a loved one. As a result, the charter of Voice of the Customer Unit indicated the goal of revising Prudential's letters, forms, statements, checks, and bills to make them simpler and more customer-focused. The group, composed of a specialized team of analysts, writers, and designers, changed the way communications are developed and was responsible for implementing these changes across the company. The team incorporated customer and agent feedback throughout every communication redesign. The group met with all of Prudential's business units to promote a stronger awareness and understanding of customers' communication needs and preferences. They reworked the content of the communications and redesigned their format, so that the new communications exhibit both cosmetic and substantive changes.

DALBAR, a research firm that ranks, evaluates, and rates written customer communications, awarded Prudential's redesigned life insurance and property and casualty bills its prestigious award, the DALBAR Seal for Communications. This marked the first time that the seal, which recognizes exceptional customer communications, was awarded to a financial services company for its billing statements. DALBAR praised the bills as being superior to any known in the industry, noting that they clearly have the customer in mind because they use plain English, are easy to understand, and are highly functional for the customer. Improving written communications is just one of the many steps Prudential is taking to enhance its relationship with its customers.

Advantage

Another example is the Advantage product that has been a tremendous success for Pruco Securities. When it was learned through feedback sessions with customers that they wanted one account for all of their personal investments and wanted to receive one statement, Prudential created the Advantage product. This product is a full-service account that offers brokerage-related products such as stocks, bonds, proprietary and nonproprietary mutual funds, unit investment trusts, certificates of deposits, and wrap accounts. It also includes money management features such as a no-fee Visa debit card, ATM access, unlimited check-writing services, an automatic bill-paying system, and automatic daily market sweeps. In addition, personal expense codes help to track expenses and assets, making tax preparation easier. All account activity is consolidated into one monthly statement. In the past eighteen months, the number of accounts has more than tripled, to 50,000. These are only two examples of how Prudential has used feedback from its customers to create products or services that will increase their satisfaction levels.[10]

Internet

Other initiatives involve providing customers with new channels for gaining access to the products and services offered by Prudential, mainly the Internet. The Internet has enormous potential for serving customers better, with richer information, interactive relationships, and innovative services. One of the benefits of serving customers online is the potential of tailoring interactive communications to fit precisely the needs of a particular person. It is critical for Prudential to utilize this medium in a way that creates and fosters loyalty among its customers. Prudential has already begun to see favorable results from the Internet strategies it has implemented, including product distribution, customer education, customer service, complaint forums, and customer quality and service questionnaires.[11]

Marketing Performance and Information Unit

To track customer satisfaction levels Prudential created the Marketing Performance and Information Unit. This group develops and utilizes standard surveys and statistical tools that facilitate the measurement of customer perceptions, attitudes, and satisfaction. The information obtained is then used to improve processes and measure success so that customer satisfaction can be increased. In addition, Prudential makes a tremendous effort to follow up with its lost customers to gain a better understanding of the drivers that caused them to leave. In many instances, a lost customer has returned simply because Prudential made the effort to contact the customer to hear what he or she had to say.[12]

Total Quality Management

Customers demand high-quality products and services and will accept nothing less. To consistently exceed expectations and satisfy their customers, many companies implement total quality management programs. Total quality management refers to the continuous improvement in quality of an organization's processes, products, and services. As Kotler points out, "higher levels of quality result in higher levels of customer satisfaction while supporting higher prices and (often) lower costs."[13] Based on an assessment completed in 2001, the National Sales Center at Prudential initiated the process to gain certification in the thirty-two areas required by the COPC-2000 Standard, modeled on the Malcolm Baldrige National Quality Award, produced by the Customer Operations Performance Center, Inc. The goal is not only to become COPC compliant but also to implement changes that will help the business achieve better results and deliver higher quality to its customers.[14]

Finally, to increase customer satisfaction, Prudential is seeking to enhance employee satisfaction. The company recognizes the important link between employee happiness and satisfaction and the positive impact this has on productivity levels and, ultimately, the customer. The company has instituted quarterly tracking surveys, employee focus groups, reward and recognition programs, a revised performance management process, and more benefits for employees. These actions have resulted in a steady improvement in employee satisfaction levels and have contributed to improved customer satisfaction levels as well.

INTERNAL CUSTOMERS

There are two sets of customers. The first includes external customers, card members, and the second, internal customers. Any company seeking to implement any type of automated system or business relationship in which the accessing of data is required needs to ensure that it is compliant with policies and standards. An internal market is seen as consisting of groups—internal customers and internal suppliers—communicating to each other within the organization. Hence, internal marketing is considered to be the process of creating market conditions within the organization to ensure that internal customers' wants and needs are met.[15]

The relationship with internal clients needs to be exactly the opposite of the relationship with external clients. Prudential is often called on to make decisions based on a business need but must always focus on the need to protect information assets.

Internal customers consist of the entire employee population. For instance, the general desktop user in any group should be able to view awareness-training materials or research information on the standards database to know what is required of him or her. This level of user does not require any direct interaction. However, employees who are creating computer systems or outsourcing work to third parties are not as easily handled. For these people, consultative services, visits, and training sessions are in order.[16]

Two of the "four P's" have played and will continue to play an important role in the success of Prudential's marketing project: "product" and "promotion." Product, that is, being able to develop a quality product, was the key focus in phase one of this initiative. Promotion now needs to take an important role. Let the market, internal clients, know what is available. Actually products will help with promotion, and promotion is facilitated by having listened to internal customers during phase one, implementing their changes and focusing on their needs.

It is effective to treat users as customers since a company's ability to achieve its goals, objectives, and mission hinges on how its employees perceive management. The group that maintained these documents prior to Security Compliance did so with little or no regard for the intended audience. To make their marketing efforts more successful, Prudential needed to invest some time in getting to know their clients.

Determining the Market

This goes beyond simply identifying internal customers; it required understanding each of the groups with which customers worked. To correctly assess a market, a company needs to break down the entire internal customer group and get to know them better. Unlike today's conventional marketing, with personalized services that try to satisfy each customer with a customized product, with a huge diverse internal customer base who all need to be served by one set of products, it is difficult to be all things to all people and find a healthy compromise that will work for everyone.[17]

PRUDENTIAL'S CABS

A CAB was the next phase of research initiated. These were "mini" advisory boards since they included only a small microcosm of the entire organization, did not include external clients, and were not conducted at some special location. However, the purpose of these meetings and the results they provided proved to be incredibly valuable. Like full-blown advisory boards, the information obtained from these meetings was worth every penny spent.

The boards were actually conducted, not on a business group level (as the surveys were), but on a personnel level. Earlier research proved that there needed to be more focus on the different levels of personnel utilizing the documents and less on the group level. Meetings were conducted at each major location, including New York, Phoenix, Montreal, Minneapolis, Salt Lake City, Fort Lauderdale, and Greensboro. Again, members were selected from the business groups that most frequently utilized the documents on the database and queried associates from all levels. The groups were formed according to staff levels. Upper management, middle management, and associate levels were all included, with colleagues at the same level but in different business groups. These sessions were treated as "rap sessions" and members were asked for complete and candid feedback from the attendees regarding their past experiences with our products: the database and the documents. Food and drink were provided and the atmosphere was "light" and "friendly" in keeping with the corporate culture. Not only did these sessions provide necessary information, but they also helped foster Security Compliance's reputation.

Results

The results of the advisory board meetings were very telling. The same results seen in the surveys also surfaced from the advisory boards; however, the details were more intimate. Having employees at each level deliver their feelings among their colleagues caused the meetings to become brainstorming sessions rather than question-and-answer sessions. It was determined at the internal board meetings that technical aspects, or "tech talk," were actually intimidating to many customers. This was true not only of clients outside of IT but also of clients within IT who aren't programmers or analysts. It became obvious that "language" was a bigger problem than initially thought.

Intimidating to many users was the feeling that, other than the actual documents, no additional guidance was available. Therefore, if they did not understand the document, they were left no other choice but to do what they thought was most effective. Another key customer service issue was that although contact numbers were listed on each document, users did not view this as appropriate support. Many users also felt that since the documents were updated so infrequently, they could not be very important; therefore, they reasoned, adherence was no longer mandatory. Tied for third place, as the most telling information from the sessions, was that many users simply did not have time to read the documents in their entirety. Since the documents contained all requirements for all users, people were often frustrated trying to search out the details that affected them and their work. Since some documents averaged forty-plus pages, most users simply gave up the search. For example, a general user who wanted to find out the minimum required password length did not want also to read about what type of security logs are required for password administration.

Prudential realized that including the audience in the project would probably be more successful than actually updating the documents. It became clear that the problem was not the product, but how it was marketed to its intended users, which made it necessary to reevaluate the format, direction, and focus of the documents, customers' needs, and the value of services. From this point forward the project became very customer service oriented.

CASE STUDY:
STRATEGIC ACCOUNT INITIATIVE, WALTER, INC.

Background

Walter, Inc., headquartered in Minneapolis, Minnesota, is a privately held international marketer, processor, and distributor of agricultural, food, financial, and industrial products and services, with some 82,000 employees in more than fifty-nine countries. After a recent restructuring, Walter, Inc., has ninety-eight business units (BUs) grouped under thirteen platforms. Approximately 50 percent of Walter, Inc., BUs market their products/services to the food industry. Each BU has its own sales force. Most BUs have a few national account salespeople. Our largest customers (Kraft/Nabisco, Nestle, General Mills/Pillsbury) have established relationships with approximately twenty to twenty-five BUs. Our strategic account management (SAM) program is just getting started.

Description

Our SAM program is in the process of being formalized. The position content summary is complete for three types of strategic account managers: full-time single account, full-time multiple accounts, and BU-sponsored accounts. We have yet to develop performance metrics and a compensation profile for SAMs and are looking to draw the "best of the best" to fill these positions.

Alternate Solution

We have traditionally looked across the company for a similar position to use as a benchmark. However, this is a new role without any set precedent.

Question

How can a CAB play a key role in measuring our strategic account initiative performance and in building a compensation program around this position?

Chapter 8

CAB Challenges for Lubrizol and Sony

A growing number of companies are exploring the question, "How can we reach outside our own four walls for the ideas we need to better serve our customers?" By systematically opening their innovation borders to customers, businesses are increasing the import and export of novel ideas. This lets companies set realistic market values for their internal ideas, helping them to better define their core businesses.[1]

Successful innovation requires the ability to harvest ideas and expertise from a wide array of sources. For a company, that means bringing in insights and know-how from outside parties. The need for external perspectives seems almost self-evident: If a company stays locked inside its own four walls, how will it be able to uncover and exploit opportunities outside its existing businesses or beyond its current technical or operational capabilities?

In an increasingly complex world, the biggest growth opportunities will come more often at the intersection of multiple companies than from visionaries acting on their own. It is important for companies to break out of their innovation boxes and find ways to link their innovation efforts. By doing this, companies can meet their customers' demands for products.[2]

INNOVATION THROUGH CUSTOMER RELATIONSHIPS

The goal is to ensure that customers have many opportunities to interact with a variety of employees in your organization, at all different levels, making it less likely that customers will perceive any one employee as indispensable. Use the following questions to evaluate your organization's customer interaction methods:

1. Do you rotate the key contact employees who serve your customers?
   - Do you have a system to expose customers to several key contact employees?
   - Have you set expectations for your customers that some rotation of key contact employees will occur but that you will make the process as seamless as possible?
   - Does information about customers reside with several employees instead of with a single key contact employee?
2. Do you use teams to serve your customers?
   - Do you use a team of employees to call on your best customers?
   - Do you make efforts to build relationships between your business customers and your outside *and inside* salespeople?
   - Do your team members have specific roles, and do your customers understand these roles?
   - If your team is hierarchical, do your customers know who the key contact employees and their backups are?
3. Besides using teams, do you cultivate multiple contacts with your customers?
   - Do you serve as a one-stop shop for customers, meeting several of their needs?
   - Do you create well-coordinated multiple contacts for different facets of your customers' businesses?
   - Are your employees required to inform others in the company about their business dealings with customers?
   - Do you create opportunities for social interactions between your customers and several employees?
4. Do you cultivate a strong corporate image in the minds of your customers?
   - Do you have a distinct corporate image beyond your employees?
   - Does your company take part in community and charitable activities?
   - Do you have strategies to promote patents and other proprietary assets or to promote your corporate citizenship or technical expertise?
5. Do you publicize the rigorous selection and hiring processes for all of your employees?
   - Do your customers know how you select and hire all of your employees?

- Do you showcase your reputation for being a highly selective employer?
- Do you tell your customers when your company is recognized as an outstanding place to work or as a family-friendly work environment?

6. Do you publicize the training you provide to key contact employees?
   - What sorts of training do you give your key contact employees? By what methods?
   - Do your customers know about the training your employees receive? How? When are they informed (before, during, or after the training)? How often?
   - When you institute new training programs for your employees, do you inform customers?
   - Do you invite key customers to attend internal training sessions held at your company that might be beneficial to them?
   - Do your customers have any input into your training programs?
   - Do you advertise the rigorousness of the training provided to your employees as a way of increasing your customers' confidence in the quality of the employees in your company?

7. Do you showcase your company's employees?
   - Do you regularly make efforts to put several of your employees in the limelight, rather than promoting just one star in your company?
   - Do you feature various employees in newsletters and annual reports?
   - Do you encourage employees to speak to business groups?
   - Do you cultivate publicity in your local media? Do you submit announcements about all personnel promotions and appointments to the press and follow up regarding their publication?
   - Do you make it known that your executives are available for speaking engagements?

8. Do your employees sufficiently understand how they should communicate your company's outstanding quality and attention to detail?
   - What do customers see when the interact with your employees?
   - Do you emphasize to your employees that appropriate attire is part of the "packaging" of employees?

- Do your employees make conscious efforts to create a sense of similarity between clients and themselves?
- Do you integrate the messages conveyed by all tangibles associated with employees—appearance and dress, brochures, business cards, and so forth?

9. When you notify customers about an impending changeover, do you provide them with a transition plan?
   - Do you demonstrate to customers that you'll do everything feasible to make the transition painless for them?
   - If available, can the previous key contact employee act as a bridge for the beginning of the transition period?
   - During the transition, is there an initial period during which new key contact employees can get acquainted with customers and begin to develop relationships without the pressure of completing day-to-day work associated with the positions?
   - Within a fairly short time after the changeover of employees, do you follow up with customers to see if they have questions or concerns about the transition or the new contact employee?

Market the succession of contacts as an opportunity to bring fresh perspectives to a problem, so customers do not question the benefit of getting to know a variety of people.

Rotation can be counterproductive if it is haphazard or overused. Instead of developing a number of strong relationships, the customer may not develop any real relationships and in fact may resent the seeming discontinuity. Most important, managers need to listen to customers.

Using teams is another way to show customers that expertise does not reside solely with a single employee. Teams can take various forms; Procter and Gamble deploys large cross-functional teams to visit its largest and most important customers, while Frito-Lay pairs junior and senior sales reps on important sales calls. Other companies partner field sales representatives with in-house staff or district managers with regional reps. Teams are also used in business-to-consumer markets.[3]

It is useful to publicize training practices since customers want to know how prepared employees are and how well they know the industry, the company, the products they are selling, and their customers. The more complex the products, processes, or customer relationships, the more customers want to know about the training. One way to showcase training is to let customers see it for themselves. Monsanto invites key customers to attend internal training sessions on technical advances and later asks customers for input on the program content, giving them a sense of partnership with Monsanto.

It makes sense to let customers know that employees are constantly retooling their skills and knowledge. Motorola is famous for its ongoing commitment to training at Motorola University, a worldwide institution with more than 100 facilities in twenty-four countries. Publicizing employees' achievements helps to put all employees in the limelight.[4]

One of the key concepts of marketing is "points of contact." A point of contact is any interaction your firm has with the public, whether in person, on the telephone, or in written communications. Every point of contact is an opportunity to form, or not form, a relationship.

Each company has both an internal and an external mission. That means three things: First, every person in a company has to be aware of, and work at, the marketing component of their job. Second, each person has to know how his or her job contributes to the external mission. Third, employees have to be empowered to further that mission.[5]

LUBRIZOL'S NEW DIRECTION AND PERFORMANCE

Lubrizol's new vision is closely tied to the environment and moving forward with new energy to become recognized as an environmental leader and advocate. The demands of the environment and ever more stringent government regulations present some of the greatest challenges faced by this industry in the twenty-first century.

Lubrizol's vision talks about making the world a better place. However, the company believes that a better world means more than cleaner air. It also means vehicles, equipment, and products that operate as they are supposed to, under tough conditions, for longer periods of time. At Lubrizol, they understand how to balance the competing demands of technology, the environment, and the marketplace so that the world is simpler and more reliable—a better place for everyone.

Perhaps the greatest benefit Lubrizol offers customers is its seven decades of experience in the science of lubricant additive chemistry. Lubrizol is in the business of solving problems, and when it comes to customers, it delivers.

In addition to additive chemistry, Lubrizol also provides a variety of services designed to make day-to-day business easier. Ordering is convenient through myLubrizol.com, its e-business initiative, which now covers Europe, North America, Asia, and Latin America. Lubrizol continues to encourage customers and strategic suppliers to connect with it electronically through the Envera network of ChemConnect, a transaction clearinghouse. ChemConnect is beginning to market some of Lubrizol's testing and blending capabilities to both traditional and new customers. Every lubricant manufacturer, no matter how large or small, is facing a world filled with unprecedented challenges.

Lubrizol's long-term investors recognize the value of market technology leadership. They appreciate the predictability and relative stability of traditional industry. Investors have voiced their support for Lubrizol's initiatives to strengthen profitability through price leadership and prudent cost management.[6]

The Gateway Additive Company was the first metalworking business Lubrizol acquired. Others, including Becker Chemie and the metalworking additive business of Alox Corporation, soon followed. In 2001, they relocated Alox's product manufacturing to Lubrizol's Painesville, Ohio, manufacturing plant. Because of the transition team's efforts, the integration was completed on schedule and under budget.

In 2001, Lubrizol made an acquisition, ROSS Chem, Inc., that opened up an important new product area. ROSS Chem specialized in defoamers, which are chemical products used in metalworking, coatings, inks, and textiles. These products are critical to fluid performance. The ROSS Chem product line complements existing Lubrizol technology and adds another dimension to its product offering.

Various Activities

Corporations, like private citizens, have a responsibility to their communities. The Lubrizol Foundation is one example of that commitment. A private foundation established in 1952, it makes grants to support a variety of educational, civic, and cultural activities. The foundation administers Lubrizol's Matching Gift Program and funds a scholarship program at thirty-seven colleges and universities.

Lubrizol encourages its employees to become actively involved in the community, especially in the area of education. Its global facilities sponsor reading and mentoring programs, school tours, and programs that encourage an appreciation of science, environmental accountability, and community responsibility. In 2001, the Lubrizol Corporation established the Lubrizol Founders Award, presented to those employees around the world who have demonstrated outstanding customer and community service. This year's recipients volunteer their time and talents in areas ranging from mentoring local school children to building houses for Habitat for Humanity.

The global growth rate for transportation lubricant additives is approximately 1 percent per year and responsible for about $18 billion in market potential. A variety of industry market forces and conditions continue to present significant challenges in this business. Among these market factors are improved engine design and longer drain intervals, industry overcapacity, frequent product specification changes, and consolidation of the customer base. Although Lubrizol is the market leader in this business, the marketplace continues to be extremely competitive.

Performance

Although Lubrizol had record shipment volume, 2001 earnings were lower than the prior year due primarily to its inability to recover higher average raw material cost. Higher operating expenses (manufacturing, selling, administrative, research, development, and testing expenses), a higher effective tax rate, a prior year gain from a litigation settlement, and special charge adjustments that did not recur in 2001 also contributed to the lower earnings.

In 2001, Lubrizol achieved record consolidated revenues of $1.84 billion, which represented an increase of $68.9 million, or 4 percent (2 percent excluding acquisitions), compared with 2000. The revenue increase was due to a 4 percent increase in shipment volume, one-half of which was due to acquisitions, including the consolidation of Lubrizol's China subsidiaries in the fourth quarter of 2000. Average additive selling price for 2001 remained flat with the prior year. This was the result of a 3 percent increase in product selling prices due to the price increases initiated during 2000 and offsetting unfavorable currency effects and product mix changes. Fluid technologies for transportation revenues increased $68.9 million, or 5 percent, compared with 2000, primarily due to increased shipment volume from acquisitions and market share gains. Fluid technologies for industry revenues were approximately the same as 2000, as the impact of the weak manufacturing sector in North America offset the additional revenues from an acquisition in 2001. The $1.0 million increase in royalties and other revenues was primarily due to increased royalties for synthetic refrigeration lubricants.

The 2001 increases over 2000 were primarily due to business gains in the engine oil additives product group in North America and strong shipments to many multinational engine oil customers in Europe. The 1 percent decrease in the Asia-Pacific region includes the favorable impact of the consolidation of China subsidiaries during the fourth quarter of 2000. Excluding China, Asia-Pacific volume would have declined 9 percent for the year, primarily due to the economic weakness in the region and some lost engine oil additive business in Japan. In Latin America, shipment volume was down due to order patterns and the economic slowdown in the region.

Gross profit (net sales less cost of sales) increased by $10.7 million, or 2 percent ($3.1 million, or less than 1 percent, excluding acquisitions), in 2001 compared with 2000 primarily for the reasons already discussed. Gross profit for fluid technologies for transportation increased by $12.6 million, or 3 percent, for 2001 compared with 2000, for the same reasons. Gross profit for fluid technologies for industry decreased by $9.7 million, or 9 percent, in 2001 compared with 2000. Excluding the impact of acquisitions, this gross profit decreased by $14.4 million, or 13 percent, primarily because the weak manufacturing sector in North America adversely affected Lubrizol's industrial additives and performance chemicals product groups.

Research, testing, and development expenses (technology expenses) increased $7.7 million, or 5 percent ($6.9 million, or 5 percent, excluding acquisitions), in 2001 compared with 2000. Product standards change periodically to meet new emissions, efficiency, durability, and other performance factors as engine and transmission designs are improved by equipment manufacturers. These changes influence the timing and the amount of technology expense. The increases during 2001 were due to high levels of testing, primarily for GF-3, which is the new U.S. passenger car motor oil technical standard, along with increased development spending for growth programs and product development costs for the next diesel engine oil specification, PC-9. Lubrizol expects PC-9 testing will continue at a high pace in the first half of 2002. During 2001, approximately 76 percent of technology costs was incurred in company-owned facilities and 24 percent was incurred at third-party testing facilities.

Lubrizol conducts a significant amount of business outside of the United States and is subject to business risks inherent in non-U.S. activities, including currency exchange rate fluctuations. While changes in the dollar value of foreign currencies will affect earnings from time to time, the longer-term economic effect of these changes should not be significant given Lubrizol's net asset exposure, currency mix, and use of U.S.-dollar-based pricing in some countries. During 2001, the U.S. dollar strengthened against most other currencies, especially the Euro and the yen, and the change in currency exchange rates had an unfavorable effect on net income as compared with exchange rates in effect during 2000.

The first program, which began in the fourth quarter of 1998, resulted in the reduction of approximately 7 percent of the workforce, or 300 employees, at both domestic and international locations. Approximately 55 percent of this reduction occurred by December 31, 1998; a further 35 percent occurred in the first quarter of 1999; and the remainder was substantially completed by the end of the third quarter of 1999. Of the 300 employees, approximately 40 percent were in the manufacturing area and 60 percent were in the selling, administrative, research, and testing areas.[7] The second program, which began in the third quarter of 1999, resulted in the additional reduction of approximately 5 percent of Lubrizol's workforce, or 187 employees, and the shutdown of twenty of Painesville's thirty-six production systems. The Painesville plant continues to operate as a producer of small-volume specialized intermediates and as a blender of certain additive packages. Lubrizol can use a CAB to understand its customers at a deep level and protect its existing key customer base (see Box 8.1). The company can also conduct a follow-up conference with these key customers at Lubrizol's offices to reinforce this deep level of partnering with its employees.

BOX 8.1. Lubrizol Advisory Board

Mission Statement: To develop policies and strategies that enable a shared vision focusing on customer needs as an integral part of future operating plans.

Vision Statement: Make Lubrizol a company where all associates support customers in ways that their unique characteristics become enablers of, rather than barriers to, corporate success and increased shareholder value.

Potential Discussion Issues

- Custom solutions
- New products
- Internal issues (organization?)
- Forum for business and industry
- Financial status of industry—How to grow profits together?
- Lubrizol market thrusts—Are they properly aligned with our core customers?
- How can we be a more efficient, effective supplier?
- How can we (Lubrizol and core customers) do better (e.g., achieve growth, other goals)?

Goals

- Lead the customer vision and mission.
- Discuss issues/challenges facing the lubricant additives industry going forward.
- Provide leadership and direction.
- Champion the customer initiative.
- Internalize customer perspectives into the Lubrizol culture, measure deliverables, and provide advisory board updates to members and executive owner.

SONY'S EXPANSION THROUGH PARTNERSHIPS AND INNOVATION

Sony Corporation headquarters is based in Tokyo, making the U.S. markets a subsidiary of the parent. Sony Corporation of America is based in New York and its principal U.S.-based businesses include Sony Electronics Corporation, Sony Pictures Entertainment, Sony Music Entertainment, and Sony Computer Entertainment America.

Sony Corporation of America is a major part of the Sony Worldwide network, recording over $17.4 billion dollars for the fiscal year ending March 31, 2001. To ensure continued success and help develop Sony Corporation of America events, Sony has announced the formation of the Sony Marketing and Event Promotion Group. The group's main purpose will be to coordinate cross-divisional marketing opportunities for Sony Corporation of America, as well as coordinate corporate-sponsored events. In addition, the group will assist in Sony Corporation's international marketing efforts and oversee Sony.Com— the U.S.-based promotional Web site. The United States is a huge market and a large part of Sony Corporation's business. Sony Corporation of America creates great exposure for the parent company through many corporate-sponsored events and through the entertainment aspects of Sony. This group's function is primarily to maximize marketing opportunities and maintain exposure in the United States.[8]

Currently, U.S. airwaves are flooded with Sony commercials and ads featuring its newest and hottest piece of audiovisual equipment, PlayStation 2 (PS2). It may seem to be just one small piece of Sony's product line, but in fact Sony derives 20 percent of its corporate revenues from PS sales. PS2 offers great opportunities for Sony, as it appeals to a particularly large age group and promises to generate revenues not only from the game consoles but for accessories and games as well. Sony has sold millions of consoles and continues to sell more and more. Chipmakers such as Toshiba and LSI Logic Corporation are supplying the chips used in the consoles, and both firms are supplying integral parts of the game console. Based on early indications of the pent-up demand, Sony has already reportedly ramped up a sizable amount of units. PlayStation 2 is expected to bring unprecedented performance to the video game player market, based on the strength of its 128-bit graphics system and high-speed memory. In addition to being backward compatible with its predecessor, the unit also features a built-in DVD player and may help fuel sales of DVD titles worldwide. Backward compatible simply means that PS2 users are able to use their old PlayStation games, which is another means of getting repeat customers. The addition of a built-in DVD player makes the console even more attractive to parents buying the PS2 console for their children, as it also makes available to them the new DVD market. AOL, the world's most famous "nontechnology" company, is believed to be negotiating a deal with Sony to run its service on the PlayStation 2. The new games console is likely to become the main platform for Internet access via a television.[9]

The move would be totally in line with AOL's must publicized "AOL Anywhere" strategy. The company recently launched a Web-based service in the United Kingdom and has stated that to date its main focus has been on the PC simply because it is the platform the majority of people use to access the Internet. While AOL has been phenomenally successful in the United States, it has yet to conquer many foreign markets. The PS2 has the potential to offer the rapid global exposure the company craves.

Unique Advantages

Sony's most admirable characteristic is its ability to be a leading producer with each new product it introduces. This is a result of Sony devotion to quality and active participation in joint ventures. Joint ventures allow companies to bring their expertise together to form a new great product and relationship. Effective October 1, 2001, Sony Corporation and Ericsson began a joint venture to create a new company that incorporates their respective mobile phone businesses worldwide. The new company, Sony Ericsson Mobile Communications, is equally owned by Ericsson and Sony, utilizing Ericsson's leading expertise in telecommunications and Sony's leading expertise in consumers electronics products.[10]

Sony Ericsson Mobile Communications is responsible for product research, design and development, as well as marketing, sales, distribution, and customer services. Ericsson and Sony, parents of the joint venture, will provide support to the new company and foster closer cooperation among all three. By combining the complementary strengths of Ericsson and Sony, the new company is uniquely positioned to become a world leader in telecommunications, as the industry moves rapidly toward Mobile Internet. These two technological power-houses appear to be a match made in heaven, with Sony bringing to the table its vast experience in consumer electronics and entertainment, and Ericsson, its mobile technology lead and the world's largest customer base among mobile operators. This is the ideal partnership for the growing market of 3G and Mobile Internet.

The mobile phone industry is fast moving toward multimedia broadband and is bound to grow significantly in the years to come.

Millions of customers will require mobile handsets that can handle smoothly and effortlessly rich content such as movies, pictures, and games, regardless of the customers' location. Through the combined efforts of Sony Corporation and Ericsson, the undisputed leader in the global telecommunications industry, the possibilities are endless.

Global corporate management for Sony Ericsson Mobile Communications is based in London and headed by Katsumi Ihara, corporate executive vice president of the joint venture. While respecting its existing product lines under the Ericsson and Sony brands, the new company will create a new and powerful brand for its range of future products. Ericsson's existing manufacturing partners and Sony's production facilities will continue to manufacture current and future products worldwide. Ericsson's Mobile Technology Platform unit will remain as a separate organization and will supply state-of-the-art technology to the new company.[11]

Partnerships and Initiatives

Another rather large joint venture that Sony took part in was with Western Digital, a leader in information storage products and services. The goal was to form a strategic partnership to codevelop hard disk drives for consumer audiovisual applications. With the arrival of the digitization of broadcasting and communications, and the convergence of audiovisual and information technology it is expected that users will require an environment that will allow personal computers and various digital audiovisual appliances to be interconnected and interoperated in an integrated home network system. The home network environment will need products such as home servers that are capable of securely storing large amounts of digital audiovisual data received from digital broadcasting and the Internet. The home server will play an important role in the home network and will enable users to enjoy quick and easy access of digital content through appliances such as televisions or personal computers. The collaborative agreement calls for Sony to develop the interface, architecture, and protocol for audiovisual applications, while Western Digital will be responsible for developing the mechanical and electronic components. Each company will contribute its respective expertise to the development effort. Sony will contribute in the areas of digital video and audio processing, and Western Digital in design and manufacturing technology.

Sony Corporation argues that its partnership with Western Digital is a strategic one, and the partnership allows Western Digital to combine its hard disk drive technology with Sony's expertise in audiovisual technology. Both companies vow to provide users with various new possibilities and forms of enjoyment in home entertainment. Western Digital Corporation is a leader in information storage products and services; it designs and manufactures hard drives for personal and enterprisewide computing—and in the future for digital audiovisual applications—and markets them to leading systems manufacturers and selected resellers under the Western Digital brand name. Western Digital is the first Fortune 500, multinational company to have been awarded companywide ISO 9001 registration, linking all Western Digital organizations with a consistent global standard for quality processes. The company was founded in 1970 and is noted for its storage and end-market systems-level design knowledge.

Various Outreach Initiatives

For the second year in a row, and the fourth time in the past six years, Sony has been picked as the best brand, according to the Harris Poll's annual survey of best brands, by Harris Interactive. Sony has achieved this, not only through its competitive edge in its marketing efforts and its entrance into new markets through its joint ventures, but also through its community relations.[12]

"Do you dream in Sony?" This key phrase represents the corporate mission of Sony: to offer the opportunity to fulfill dreams to all kinds of people involved with Sony. Those people consist of the stakeholders, employees, customers, shareholders, and the community. Sony created Community Relations (CR) activities to ensure the mission's success by obtaining donations of money and products and encouraging volunteer work by employees and involvement in other activities and programs. The company understands its social responsibility as a global company as not only to develop products and technology but to support the community in various ways. The CR activities create value to the community as well as enhance the corporate brand value and reputation.

The CR activities possess an "integrated and decentralized" management style that reflects the corporate vision of the Sony Group. In integrated and decentralized management business units and group companies with enhanced independence and autonomy influence one another, creating new value. In this structure, the CR is responsible for coordinating (integrating) the independent (decentralized) activities developed and performed by the group companies. Consideration is given to the needs of the local communities and involves helping the group companies to create partnerships with local groups. Each individual group is primarily responsible for the creation and implementation of its CR activities. The CR foundations in the United States, Canada, Europe, Australia, Asia, and Africa have unique features tailored to the needs of their communities.

Corporate Culture

Sony's emphasis on respect for the individual and on each person's uniqueness is reflected in its corporate culture. In turn, Sony places a priority on education for children. Sony is aware of its social responsibility to contribute to the development of communities. With this in mind, Sony strives to improve the quality of education. Sony uses its strengths to bring education to children in South Africa via the School TV Access Project. This project uses the public broadcaster to produce the country's first educational program for elementary school students. Sony also addresses the problems of poverty and other social issues brought about by the widening gap in living standards. Globalization has its dark side, and Sony, fully cognizant of its responsibility to society, supports community-level human development activities. The Sony Asia Fund helps Indonesian nonprofit organizations to provide learning opportunities for children. Sony works to become a corporate citizen through its global activities. It takes on the role of global localization by respecting the culture and customs of the community and acting as a local company in every market it enters by donating and participating in the culture, welfare, and educational activities of the community.[13]

Sony also focuses on the internal cooperation and conservation of the environment. Although the environmental activities are not a part of the CR activities, they play a major role in Sony's vision to helping communities and society. Sony created the Corporate Environmental

Risk Management Guideline to ensure that its manufacturing processes pose little harm to the environment. The Corporate Environmental Risk Management Guidelines were created by an international working group of representatives from America, Europe, Asia and the headquarters in Japan to set up clear, simple, practical procedures, making use of existing ISO 14001 EMS (Environmental Management Systems). ISO 14001 is an international standard for environmental management systems. Sony also attained at thirty-five manufacturing sites "zero landfill," defined as a reduction of waste generated in landfills by reducing or recycling more than 95 percent of the waste generated. Sony has set goals to broaden the range of the environmental procedures to include R&D, product design, production processes, management of sites, repair services, distribution, marketing, and customer services.

Risk Management

Sony's guidelines for environment risk management consist of risk assessment, risk control, and emergency communication. A simple matrix (Table 8.1) was created to successfully, and as accurately as possible, assess risk. The matrix (risk × probability) was developed using data from chemical consumption and risk protection measures on the site. Risk control pertains to monitoring and alarm systems, procedures, emergency drills, and so on, in the event of a risk emergency. An emergency communication plan was set up to ensure immediate and proper crisis communication in an unavoidable event of an environmental accident. A contact list is established—who is to speak, what media will report, and where a conference will take place if need be. Sony understands the importance of risk management, es-

TABLE 8.1. Risk Management Matrix

Risk Assessment	Risk Control	Emergency Communication
Simple matrix	Facility criteria	Contact list
Risk × probability	Emergency preparedness	Contents
	Audit Program, utilizing ISO 14001 EMS	

pecially due to the fact that they regularly deal with hazardous and wasteful materials. The creation of the Corporate Environmental Risk Management Guidelines is a way for Sony to successfully prepare for an emergency and effectively address the crisis.

Sony Performance

Sony helps make many lives more enjoyable through its electronic products, music, and pictures, but it also has a responsibility to its consumers, shareholders, employees, and the communities in which it operates to create little harm to the environment. It is also the responsibility of Sony to be prepared to address a crisis in the event one occurs. Sony recorded consolidated annual sales of over $58.5 billion for the fiscal year ending March 31, 2001, and it employs 181,800 people worldwide. Sony Corporation of America recorded over $17.4 billion in sales in the United States for the fiscal year ending March 31, 2001. The company is one of the most comprehensive businesses in the world, providing products/services in music, motion pictures, television, computer entertainment, and online businesses. Sony has successfully remained the leading audiovisual electronics and information technology company in the United States and worldwide by providing products such as digital cameras, handy camcorders, personal stereos, and computers. It is among the leading music, motion picture, and television production companies in the United States and worldwide. Sony is the codeveloper of the CD and DVD, as well as manufacturer and marketer of PlayStation. Sony is publicly held, with shares listed on sixteen stock exchanges worldwide, including Tokyo, New York, and London.

Challenges

Sony has diversified its business into numerous successful departments, all which are independent of one another.[14] It has entered over fifty markets and set up R&D and manufacturing facilities all over the world. However, with all of its success Sony does face some major competition in the game console industry. Microsoft's Xbox is predicted to command more than a quarter of the game market by the end of next year and surpass the market share of Sony's PlayStation 2 by the end of 2003. If that happens, it would give Microsoft the wedge it needs to play a central part in home entertainment apart from the personal computer. The Xbox also works as a DVD player and has a hard drive and an Ethernet connection port on the back suitable for a cable modem or a digital subscriber line Internet connection. Although the Xbox costs roughly $150 more than PlayStation 2, it offers Internet connection to play against others on the Web.

One method for Sony to remain the leader of the game console industry is to focus its attention on game selection. The Xbox is new to the industry and currently offers only five to ten games. Sony, on the other hand, offers numerous games, from Tony Hawk's ProSkater 3 to Madden NFL 2002. PlayStation should continue to create new, exciting, and surreal games that will soar above the Xbox selection. In the meantime, PlayStation 3 should be in the works. Sony needs to create a version that connects to the Internet and add some new features, such as the ability to download music and games from a Sony Web site.

Sony also needs to continue to enter new markets. Sony is opening the first Japanese manufacturing and selling company of personal computers in China. Still, in many markets Sony has not gained its full potential due to its costly high-tech products. Through Sony's CR activities the company is able to help build communities that will in the future obtain the knowledge to use the products offered by Sony. Sony should concentrate its efforts into developing a stronger educational system in the less developed countries to ensure growth in those communities, which will not only further the development in those countries but also help Sony in the long run. Sony also needs to develop a CAB to help in its partnerships with its customers so it can stay current with marketplace changes. This will also allow Sony to develop new products, add value for customers, and provide fast technology for its client base.

CASE STUDY: LUBRIZOL AND SONY

Lubrizol is currently experiencing very intense competitive challenges. While they are performing fine, they are concerned about losing key customers, market share, and augmenting sales penetration. Likewise, Sony has experienced downsizing, layoffs, and management cuts and is concerned about being more responsive to its customers and the marketplace. How can both organizations develop a CAB to face and overcome their competitive challenges?

Chapter 9

Global Applications

Corporations utilize CABs for different reasons, e.g., to ensure a successful future by incorporating customers' needs with the exchange of ideas, issues, and concerns into a clientele networking system. The forum is useful in providing feedback to account associates in management teams. Many enterprises, such as those related to the Internet, real estate, e-business, airlines, investment agencies, networks, restaurant chains, and customer service centers, employ CABs. Some examples are Radiant Systems, Vancouver Tourism, Island Data, Mazu Networks, Northwest Airlines, Delta Airlines, Akamai, and Vicinity Corporation.

REAL-WORLD CABS

Radiant Systems

Radiant Systems had established its Rapid Fire Customer Advisory Board to incorporate customer input of concerns and needs into its management team. Radiant Systems does this to form a rigid customer base among fifteen customers to achieve ultimate success.

Radiant Systems utilizes a roster method for referencing that entails a list of restaurant proprietors' names, their company names, and e-mail addresses. Clients have two ways of providing feedback directly to their account associate. One would be to fill out a software enhancement form or to contact one of the leisure CAB members. This is an excellent way for the owner to incorporate customer suggestions into everyday business activity.

Some constraints of the board are that the board positions are held for only a two-year term. Membership is limited to all restaurant owners who use the Rapid Fire system in one or more of their locations. Board openings are available only during an "open" period or when a vacancy occurs.

Vancouver Tourism

Vancouver Tourism's program consists of an assortment of leading-edge customer service and value-added customer benefits, gathering decision makers and addressing event issues such as clientele communication, technology deployment, housing, and relationship building. Vancouver's top professionals are from diversified places of the world, for example, the United States, Japan, Germany, the United Kingdom, and Canada. These countries provide Vancouver with input based on their differing degrees of experience in the different countries. This expertise helps Vancouver to dispense the best, most up-to-date melange of customer services and destination value anywhere in the world.

Vancouver is purposeful in offering tourism convention-planning services such as

- site inspection,
- attendance building,
- accommodation services, and
- meeting services.

Site inspection encompasses the location of Vancouver's Spectacular City located in British Columbia, Canada, with accommodation arrangements and airport transfers. Site Board of Directors hosts the Board of Directors meeting, offering complimentary accommodations, airport transfers, car rental advantages, airline bookings, and pre- and postmeeting activities.

Attendance building is Vancouver's promotional activity for requesting Vancouver as a destination at one of the company's annual meetings the year prior to a company meeting in Vancouver. Vancouver will provide a company with promotional literature, posters, postcards, video, or slides to increase customer company awareness.

The following are a few of the *accommodation services* offered by Vancouver:

- *Group booking agreement*—a prototype in North America. The group booking agreement is linked with Vancouver's convention hotels to the common contract standards for cut-off dates, attrition, and other imperative clauses.

- *Housing provider*—"high tech and high touch," providing superb quality of convention delegate and event housing. It also sustains elevated service standards and efficient and cost-effective applications, encircling online housing reservations.
- *Exchange rate program*—advantageous for delegates. They receive a preferred exchange rate at all bank locations as a result of Vancouver's relationship with the Royal Bank of Canada.
- *Customized welcome signage*—offered by Vancouver's Tourist Info Center. Member storefronts customize welcome signs, which are then distributed community-wide to familiarize company delegates and their meetings.

Greatest of all, Vancouver permits its customers to keep in touch with top management by providing a staff member contact list, which contains different regional areas of the world.

Island Data

Another customer service provider is Island Data Corporation. Island Data provides services to its customers via a different approach than Vancouver. Island Data offers leading resolutions to an online customer service market. Its CAB convention's motto was "Maximizing the Value of Your Online Customer Service Solution."

Island Data is an integral component in RealNetworks, Inc. RealNetworks assisted Island Data in maximizing the value of their online automated response solution. In return, Island Data's CAB took a role in RealNetworks' efforts to consistently overcome their customer complacency for more than 180 million RealPlayer users.

Island Data's CAB exists as a customer group designed to give input and feedback to Island Data's flagship automated response solution Express Response. The meetings featured discussions on a category of topics related to the customer relationship management (CRM) industry. Members of the board determined that their end users need facilitated and expedient access to expert knowledge, and that user-facing automated support systems should be a constituent of their online customer services efforts. Members exchanged strategic tactics that have supported them in becoming more customer focus oriented, with customer satisfaction via the online interaction experience a primary goal. Members also offered insights on how Express Response can help make the Q&A more personal for the user.

Other CAB meeting goals of Island Data entail giving input to future product development activities, achieving maximum return on investment (ROI) from automated response systems, maximizing the value of knowledge in management, and sharing success stories about and challenges to effective customer support.[1]

Island Data Corporation converts online customer service and support into a strategic customer loyalty and retention tool. This is done by fast, accurate, relevant, and personalized responses to customers' electronic inquiries and is achieved with substantial cost savings in call center operations. Island Data integrates all electronic communication channels, interpreting unstructured inquires and leveraging its existing business knowledge to automatically distribute personalized responses to online user inquiries in seconds.

Mazu Networks, Inc.

Mazu Networks, Inc., a networks technology company, works to circumvent denial of service (DOS) attacks and other threats to e-business growth. Mazu's customer advisory board was shaped through three enterprise-computing industry leaders: Bowstreet, Inc., Storage Networks, Inc., and PSINet, Inc.

Mazu forms business webs, which positions Mazu to conform to the growing customer demand for carrier-class Internet security services. Customers will be able to make their networks smarter and more proactive in addressing DOS attacks as a network availability problem. Mazu provides a solution to enable the network infrastructure so that Internet and network service providers are able to thwart one of the most whimsical threats to their customer relationships and service-level agreements.

Mazu's first solution to resolve the issue is to detect, deflect, and inevitably disarm DOS attacks with the application of high-performance and innovative packet analysis technologies. Once this is put into effect then customers can enable themselves to build a better network. Mazu provides a network that is more flexible, configurable, and highly resistant to attacks.

Northwest Airlines

Northwest Airlines has been recognized by the Department of Transportation for being the most on-time U.S. airline among the seven leading carriers for nine consecutive years and for its increased attention to the concerns of passengers with disabilities.

Northwest's CAB is part of its Customer First service plan and consists of ten members. The company's CAB has different local and national disability and advocacy organizations representing it, some of which are Self Help for Hard of Hearing People, Inc. (SHHH), the National Association of the Deaf, Inc., Consortium for Citizens with Disabilities, and Amigo Mobility International, Inc. Northwest's advisory board provides the company with suggestions on how the airline can better serve and communicate with the expanding travel segment of passengers with disabilities. Board members serve a brief one-year term and convene on a quarterly basis to revise Northwest's present and proposed policies and procedures along with training programs related to services. A quote from Northwest Executive Vice President and Chief Operating Officer Richard Anderson exemplifies the company's optimistic attitude: "Our goal with the advisory board and with the extensive training and procedure review we've implemented with our Customers First program is to offer the best customer service in the industry." In 2000, Northwest was the recipient of the Air Transport World Airline Technology Management Award. Northwest also won a popularity vote from *Inside Flyer Magazine* and readers of *Time in Asia*.[2]

Delta Airlines

Delta Airlines' advisory board specializes in customers with specific needs. Delta Airlines and Northwest Airlines are very comparable in terms of tailoring to customers with disabilities, and they also are close rivals. In conjunction with Delta Airlines, the Paralysis Society of America and Seeing Eye, Inc., offer guidance on serving passengers with disabilities.

The motives of the board are to provide the airline with advice on how to cater to customers with specific needs, appoint certain individual employees to oversee the progression of the programs, improve communication among employees, and update them on novel provisions and business practices. Employee training is imperative to the enhancement of quality service to passengers with disabilities.

The company currently offers travelers with special needs travel guide brochures that are available in large print, Braille, and audio.

Akamai Technologies, Inc.

Akamai Technologies, Inc., is the leading provider of distributed application and content delivery services. These services permit companies to reduce the complexity and cost of deploying and operating a uniform Web infrastructure, ensuring unmatched performance, reliability, scalability, and manageability. Services provided by Akamai give businesses a distinct competitive advantage and offer an incomparable Internet experience for their customers. Akamai also operates in fifty-six countries. Active members of Akamai's CAB are Accenture, Apple, BET Interactive, Barnes&Noble.com, CNET Networks, iClips, IFILM, Macromedia, McAfee, Merck, The Motley Fool, MTVi, Nike, SAKS Direct, Ticket Master, and Washingtonpost.Newsweek Interactive. Akamai's customer base is comprised of businesses leveraging the Internet to deliver engaging and vibrant content, streaming media, interactivity, and a stimulating user experience. This enhances brand image and drives e-commerce revenues. The CAB returns feedback and user analysis that have aided with the creation of Akamai's innovative services.

One of Akamai's most vital goals as a company is to become a strategic partner for each of its customers. Chairman and CEO George Conrades believes that, to achieve this, Akamai must excel as a service provider and lead the market in providing technology solutions that conform to real business necessities. Akamai originated its CAB in 2000 to gain a better understanding of the business requirements of its more than 1,400 customers through close interaction with a meticulously selected representative group. Members of Akamai Customer Advisory Board meet monthly throughout the year to talk about strategic updates on products and services.

Vicinity Corporation

Vicinity is the first in a new category of "enterprise location services" vendors to help global, multilocation companies effectively harness the power of location intelligence. Vicinity unifies and enriches Web, wireless, and speech inquiries to catalyze a fundamental improvement in the customer experience. Vicinity turns location information into a coherent, rich source of knowledge and embeds location intelligence into the fabric of the organization.

Vicinity Corporation recently established a twenty-member Vicinity Customer Advisory Board. Members of Vicinity's CAB include McDonald's, Wells Fargo, CitiBank, Best Western International, Domino's Pizza, Starwood Hotels and Resorts, Equiva (Shell and Texaco), Hertz Europe, Ericsson, Harley-Davidson, Bank of America, Royal Dutch Shell, Kinko's, FedEx, US Bank, and U.S. Bancorp Piper Jaffray. Attendees from these companies hold various e-business, IT, and CRM senior executive positions.

Vicinity's customer base consists of global, multilocation organizations that recognize the importance of managing location information and the customer experience. These organizations operate thousands of locations, many with unique characteristics and attributes that change frequently. The Vicinity CAB provides feedback on the proposed direction Vicinity is taking relative to its products and services. Vicinity developed the CAB as a means to gather input on its more than 310 customers' business requirements, and to incorporate that input into future products and services.

This board believes in the importance of enterprise location services and how they benefit the entire organization. Through the Vicinity CAB, the company is able to discuss the technologies that help shape enterprise location services and what will benefit each industry. Vicinity sees the importance of reaching its customers with important individual station services and location information. Vicinity values its customers' input on the current and future development of enterprise location services, believing it to be an essential part of the process of understanding customers' needs.

COMPETITIVE ADVANTAGE IN INTERNATIONAL MARKETS

Global competitiveness is predicated on creating strong interorganizational networks. Successful development and administration of interorganizational networks is derived from effective intercultural communication efforts focused on developing relationships. The ability of an organization to identify, maintain, and strategically build interorganizational networks for the mutual benefit of network members and for the reduction of dysfunctional relational outcomes has been the underlying strategy of many organizations in globalizing their operations.[3] The success of business relationships over the long run is contingent on each partner's investment in each network relationship as well as the partners' ability to communicate effectively throughout the direction of the relationship.[4] The competitive importance of strong relationships has generated an underlying paradigm shift in marketing and organizational strategy that has redefined the exchange process.[5]

Second, stronger, more intimate relationships increase the effectiveness of the interorganizational network, thereby differentiating it from less well-coordinated competitive networks. Therefore, firms with relationship networks can provide enhanced services to existing customers as well as more attractive services and benefits compared with competitors that do not have ongoing relationships. To reap the benefits of strong relational networks in the global marketplace, effective interorganizational communications need to be established among members of the network.

Building a sustainable competitive advantage is widely viewed as a key factor underlying an effective marketing strategy.[6] Relatively little attention has been centered on how an individual firm can or should craft a sustainable competitive advantage in international markets. (See Box 9.1 for a list of criteria necessary for global business success.) Typically, it is assumed that the firm can succeed by leveraging its domestic positioning, for example, through a cost leadership, differentiation, or niche strategy in international markets.[7] As a result, in assessing its overall competitive advantage in global markets, a firm needs to consider the strengths and weaknesses of its competitive positions in each country's market and how these interact to influence deployment of resources worldwide. The following examples illustrate this issue.

Distinctive capabilities are the foundation of a firm's position in the marketplace. In assessing whether these capabilities can be transferred to international markets to provide the firm with a sustainable competitive advantage, two important issues must be considered. The first is the extent to which the markets targeted are characterized by distinctive customer needs and interests, competitors, and market in-

---

BOX 9.1. Criteria for Successful Global Sales

If you are involved in global markets what do you think it takes to conduct a successful global sales effort?

- Proven technology, technical comprehension, quality products, service, delivery, and price
- Trust
- Effective communication and commitment for the long term; sales and marketing having a cohesive strategy yet understanding different markets have different needs
- Same sell language, joint ownership of account; same compensation plan and industry segmentation helpful
- Analysis—complete and thorough information, cultural sensitivity, and government and economic savvy
- Coordination of sales centers
- Common goals, communication with all involved, pricing in each country's exchange rate, feedback mechanism, and leader for account
- Strong branding, united message, operating systems/software that allows communication and sharing of data
- Product definition, market segmentation, sales support, sales training, recruiting
- Real globalization—multinational workforce—When you stop talking about culture being a "problem," you are OK!
- Overcoming cultural difference, applying different leadership styles according to situations, certain business practices, salespeople with global skills

---

frastructure and separated by economic, political, and cultural barriers. These distinctive aspects may require the firm to tailor its position and adapt or develop distinctive capabilities to meet specific local needs. The second pertains to how far assets and capabilities are location-specific; for example, production techniques or processes may be adapted to a given cultural environment with specific labor or management skills. Channel-bonding processes may be tailored to distribution systems in which channel relationships are built on trust and commitment.

As international market expansion becomes a key priority for an increasing number of firms, formulating a strategy to compete effectively in global markets becomes critical to success. The firm needs to establish a strong competitive position in a broad range of markets relative to local and regional competitors as well as to other firms operating globally. In building a global competitive position, it is important to consider the spatial configuration of assets and resources and to assess not only similarities and differences among markets in different geographic locations but also the patterns of market interdependence and the forces driving toward greater market integration.[8]

In many cases in which markets are geographically dispersed and independent, the firm will need to compete across multiple diverse markets, modifying its positional advantage to local market characteristics and competitor posture. At the same time, mechanisms to coordinate these positions will need to be developed—through improved harmonization and integrating and linking activity systems across markets. Often this leads to the development of border-spanning capabilities that provide the firm with a competitive advantage in managing activity systems in international markets.

THE NATURE OF GLOBAL RELATIONS

Globalization is destroying the last remnants of stewardship for natural resources in industries such as forest products. Today, buy-and-sell decisions are executed by faceless agents living on the other side of the world from the people and ecosystems whose futures they decide. Moreover, new economy growth stimulates related growth in old economy industries—along with the familiar pattern of suburban sprawl, pollution, loss of habitat, and competition for natural resources.

The new economy's effects on social capital are more complex but no less disturbing. Industrial progress has tended to destroy cultural as well as biological diversity, despite the protests of marginalized groups such as the Provençal farmers who oppose the globalization of food production. Likewise, although changes in traditional family and community structures have brought greater freedom for women and many ethnic groups, the past decade also has brought worldwide increases in divorce rates, single-parent families, and "street" children. Global markets, capital flows, and e-commerce open up new opportunities for emerging economies, but they also create new generations of technological haves and have-nots.

Many companies have attempted to build learning organizations with little grasp of the depth of the changes required. They want to increase imagination and creativity without unleashing the passion that comes from personal vision. They seek to challenge established mental models without building real trust and openness. They espouse systems thinking, without realizing how threatening that can be to established "quick fix" management cultures. There is a difference between building more sustainable enterprises because there is profit in it and because it is one's life's work. The journey ahead will require both.

If understanding natural systems establishes the guiding ideas for sustainability innovations, then learning provides the means to translate ideas into accomplishments. The logic of a learning culture conflicts with traditional, control-oriented organizational cultures. To a controlling culture, a learning culture based on passion, curiosity, and trust appears to be out of control. This does not make life easier for people in organizations; it makes it more demanding—but also more exciting. Today, it is important to understand customers and serve their genuine needs. The shift from "the value is in the stuff" to "the value is in the service the stuff provides" also may lead to a radical shift in the concept of ownership.

How a company thinks of itself in relation to its customers should involve providing value *for* customers as well as obtaining value *from* customers. As Volvo discovered years ago, when a company is only selling cars, its relationship with the customer ends with the purchase. When it is providing customer satisfaction, it just begins. Focusing on the services provided by products also shifts the very meaning of *customer.* Customers are no longer passive; they are cocreators of value (see Figure 9.1).

Activist customers think for themselves and activist customers are organizing themselves using the market as a forum. People who are coinnovating must know each other and trust each other—in ways unnecessary in traditional relationships between providers and customers.

Intense cooperative learning will never occur unless companies view their fates as linked. That is why the shift from seeing a world of suppliers and customers to one in which "we are all part of larger systems" is essential. Companies that do not recognize their interdependence with customers will never build the trust needed to shift established mental models. The world in which key corporate decisions could be made behind closed doors is disappearing.

A NEW VIEW OF CUSTOMER VALUE

Traditional product view

"Lifetime value of a new customer" view

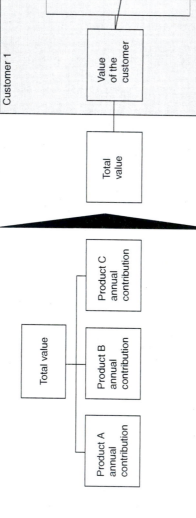

FIGURE 9.1. Customer relationship building is based on global customer value.

SABA'S GLOBAL CAB

Saba is the leading provider of human capital development and management (HCDM) solutions that consist of Internet-based learning, performance, content and resource management systems, business-to-business exchanges, integrated content, and related services. Customers around the world rely on Saba for HCDM infrastructure to increase competitive advantage by rapidly building critical skills throughout their extended enterprise of customers, partners, employees, and suppliers.

Global 2000 customers include Medtronic, Anheuser-Busch, Cisco Systems, Ford Motor Company, DaimlerChrysler, General Electric, Veritas Software, EMC Corporation, Sun Microsystems, Planet, Red Hat, Hyundai, 3Com, the Competence Network of Norwegian Business and Industry, and the U.S. Veterans Benefits Administration. Founded in 1997, Saba is a global company headquartered in Redwood Shores, California.

Saba announced the formation of a global customer advisory board (GCAB) made up of key Saba customers representing a broad spectrum of the Saba Global 2000 customer base. The GCAB is an independent, self-governing body with the mission of working with Saba to set directions and give guidance about Saba products, features, functionality, and market direction.[9]

The GCAB meets on a quarterly basis and covers an agenda that includes Saba product and service offerings. This established customer community works to collect, assemble, and present information to Saba to build product and service offerings that correspond to the needs of Saba customers. Saba is a nonvoting participant, attending on an invited basis.

The GCAB is committed to listening to and learning from Saba's customers to ensure the validity of Saba's corporate and product direction, and that the company is delivering the most value-added solutions to its customers. The GCAB will enhance Saba's ability to learn from customers more quickly, get an edge on the competition, and continue to build a leadership position in next-generation management solutions.

The GCAB will enable Saba customers to leverage this formalized structure and learning forum to infuse the customer voice within Saba. As the GCAB evolves, regional user groups and special interest groups will form to empower collaboration among peers, sharing of best practices, and addressing the challenges of implementing e-learning solutions. The GCAB will focus on some of the specific e-learning challenges and trends seen today by organizations worldwide, including developing and retaining employees; aligning and enhancing competencies across the extended enterprise of customers, partners, employees, and suppliers; ensuring regulatory compliance; integrating multiple and fragmented training registration and tracking systems; moving toward "blended learning" approaches; and linking learning to workforce planning and performance management.

GLOBAL INTEGRATION OF STRATEGIC CHANGE

PricewaterhouseCoopers

The management consulting services practice of Pricewaterhouse-Coopers helps global and national clients maximize their business performance through seamless integration of strategic change, process improvements, and technology solutions. Combining the talents and skills of 25,000 people worldwide, PricewaterhouseCoopers consultants manage complex projects with global capabilities and local expertise, from strategy through implementation. PricewaterhouseCoopers' global network is the world's largest professional services organization, with more than 140,000 people in 152 countries.

PricewaterhouseCoopers has become a member of the Open Applications Group, Inc. (OAGI), a nonprofit industry consortium comprised of the world's leading business software applications companies. PricewaterhouseCoopers has also been appointed to the OAGI board and will oversee operations of the organization's CAB, responsible for ensuring that customer and vendor priorities are well reflected by the OAGI's activities.[10] In joining the organization, PricewaterhouseCoopers will become active in assisting the OAGI achieve its primary mission: promoting easy and cost-effective integration of key business-application software components. The OAGI addresses all areas of an enterprise application portfolio with the goal of enhancing integration integrity while driving down the ongoing cost of application ownership.

The OAGI

The OAGI is the leading business-application software vendor association in the world. It advances industry awareness of issues and solutions regarding interoperability of business components through the development and publication of a common specification that defines the dialogues required to integrate these components.

The Open Applications Group Integration Specification (OAGIS) defines interapplication integration scenarios and details the message formats required for connecting the applications. The OAGIS encompasses interoperability specifications for front-office, back-office, and supply chain business software components, including financial, human resources, manufacturing, supply chain, and logistics applications.

Coombe Women's Hospital

In Ireland, government health policies have expressed a desire to give women a greater say in the type and quality of health care they receive. Coombe Women's Hospital is involved in the provision of health care services to women and their "customers" are patients and their families. As a large women's hospital delivering in excess of 6,000 babies per annum (13 percent of the national births), they strive to provide a quality service. In an attempt to be sensitive to the needs of its "customers," this hospital has had a Patients Advisory Council (PAC) for a number of years. Twelve members, who are all previous maternity service customers of the hospital, meet with the master (chief executive officer) up to five times per year. The PAC allows the service providers at the hospital to be sensitive not only to the current needs but also the evolving needs of patients and their families. A number of modifications to the existing service have been the direct result of recommendations from this committee.

The council has also proved useful as a sounding board for new ideas and strategies. One such strategy was the design of a measurement instrument to evaluate customer satisfaction with the maternity service at the hospital. The PAC, together with patients on the wards, helped to determine the dimensions of quality in the maternity service that should be measured. Patients were also involved in the wording and design of the questionnaire used. The involvement of customers both in an advisory capacity and in the development of an ongoing satisfaction survey enabled the hospital to determine the needs, priorities, and satisfaction levels of its customers, a strategy designed by customers for customers.[11]

Lucent Technologies

Customers' needs and wants are important drivers in any product development at Lucent Technologies, but the server project went a step beyond the usual. Customers became, in a real sense, part of the design team. Before the server was fully defined, more than 100 customers from around the world participated in focus groups. The resulting observations helped the design team set priorities on which features their offering would include. In addition, early prototyping in a concept trial conducted by the McDonald's Corporation yielded valuable real-world experience that influenced the product.

Then, a customer advisory council (CAC) was formed. Its members were customers with two things in common: all had work groups that shared applications and needed to communicate voice, video, and images across local- and wide-area networks, and all saw how multimedia communications would add value to their business operations. In selecting CAC members with motivated interest in multimedia products, Lucent Technologies' objective was to develop a customer-defined product that could be tested and evaluated by those who had defined it.

The twelve CAC members met—and still meet—in monthly audio-video conferences with the marketing and development team. They receive reviews of the product's status and information on how their feedback has been used. Many aspects of today's server stem from the work of CAC members. Here are some examples: Customers thought it would be natural to start all calls with voice, then allow other media to be implemented, which is how the server works. Customer requirements defined the workstation platforms supported by the first release of the server. Because of CAC suggestions, plans were formulated to support PCs as end points for the next immediate release. Customers wanted the ability to have a virtual meeting room set up prior to a conference. The direct result is that the whiteboard and other features can be ready to go even before the call is made. Though many sophisticated video controls can be provided, customers insisted on simplicity. The final design, offering a carefully selected subset of possible options, reflects their wishes.[12]

The CAC, in a general sense, proved the positive value of establishing open communications between a product-definition team and the product's ultimate customers. It also was an invaluable help in crystallizing the marketing approach to multimedia because its members conveyed a clear understanding of how the server would be used in their businesses.[13]

CONCLUSION

Highly skilled managers and sales professionals should always explore and use competitive tools. CABs are one of the most efficient, successful strategic competitive tools available to organizations. By developing a personalized dialogue with buyers on an ongoing basis and listening to their needs, concerns, and feedback organizations can become more responsive, insightful, and competitive. It is important that an organization acts on the members' input at some level, even if it does not adopt every suggestion the CAB may have made. This demonstrates a sincere and secure organization willing to listen to critical feedback from clients because it genuinely cares and understands them.

CASE STUDY: ORGANIZATIONAL TEAMWORK, FRENCH AIRWAYS WORLD CARGO

Synopsis

A "key account" team was introduced to the Americas Sales Team six months ago.

We have just got to the phase in their development where they are "flexing their muscles." Sales managers are complaining that the key account team members are making national decisions that impact their local results without consultation/agreement. The key account team members are complaining that they have "no teeth" (they are a more senior grade than sales managers and just want to "pull rank").

Background

French Airways World Cargo (FAWC) is an operating division of French Airways. Its "mission" is to fill the bellyholds of FA passenger aircraft with freight, at a return that outweighs the marginal cost of selling, handling, and flying the freight to its destination. The Americas sales team includes 100 outside and inside salespeople in Canada, the United States, Latin America, and the Caribbean. The key account team includes three sales directors who liaise with the head offices of freight forwarders (our primary customers) and therefore are accountable for driving revenue across some/all sales areas.

Headline Problem

We need the most effective organizational relationship to ensure that the key account team and sales management team work effectively as an "Americas Commercial Team."

Question

What different approaches using a CAB could help "smooth the path" to ensure that the team works together consistently and effectively?

Notes

Chapter 1

1. M. Campanelli, What Price Sales Force Satisfaction? *Sales and Marketing Management Magazine* 146(7) (July 1994), p. 37.

2. A. Kohn, Why Incentive Plans Cannot Work, *Harvard Business Review* 71(5) (September-October 1993), pp. 54-63.

3. A. Kohn, Breaking with Tradition, *Sales and Marketing Management Magazine* 146(6) (June 1994), p. 94.

4. G. Trumfio, What's Your Vision? *Sales and Marketing Management Magazine* 146(6) (June 1994), p. 41.

5. J. Hanson and D. Krackhardt, Informal Networks: The Company Behind the Chart, *Harvard Business Review* 71(4) (July-August 1993), pp. 104-111.

6. J. Pereira, Bosses Will Do Almost Anything to Light Fires Under Salespeople, *The Wall Street Journal* (April 27, 1993), p. B1.

7. T. Carter, *Contemporary Sales Force Management* (Binghamton, NY: The Haworth Press, 1998).

8. N. Capon, *Marketing in the 21st Century* (Englewood, NJ: Prentice-Hall, 2001).

9. T. C. Kinnear, A Perspective on How Firms Relate to Their Markets, *Journal of Marketing* 63(1) (1999), pp. 112-114.

10. C. Moorman and R. T. Rust, The Role of Marketing, *Journal of Marketing* 63(1) (1999), pp. 180-197.

11. T. Carter, Cultivation Council, *Selling Power* 19(3) (May 1999), pp. 100-102.

Chapter 2

1. D. Ray, Bank on Trust, *Selling Power* 19(2) (March 1999), p. 22.

2. J. Cannon and C. Homburg, Buyer-Supplier Relationships and Customer Firm Cost, *Journal of Marketing* 65(1) (January 2001), p. 29.

3. R. Bagozzi and U. Dholakia, Goal Setting and Goal Striving in Consumer Behavior, *Journal of Marketing* 63 (Special Issue 1999), p. 19.

4. R. Oliver, Whence Customer Loyalty, *Journal of Marketing* 63 (Special Issue 1999), p. 33.

5. R. Achrol and P. Kotler, Marketing in a Network Economy, *Journal of Marketing* 63 (Special Issue 1999), p. 146.

6. R. Srivastava, T. Shervani, and L. Fahey, Marketing Activities and the Discipline of Marketing, *Journal of Marketing* 63 (Special Issue 1999), p. 168.

7. C. Moorman and R. Rust, The Role of Marketing, *Journal of Marketing* 63 (Special Issue 1999), p. 180.

8. T. Gruen, J. Summers, and F. Acito, Relationship Marketing Activities, Commitment and Membership Behaviors in Professional Associations, *Journal of Marketing* 64(3) (July 2000), p. 34.

9. D. Stewart, Beginning Again: Change and Renewal in Intellectual Communities, *Journal of Marketing* 63(4) (October 1999), p. 2.

10. S. Fournier and D. Mick, Rediscovering Satisfaction, *Journal of Marketing* 63(4) (October 1999), p. 5.

11. L. Price and E. Arnold, Commercial Friendship: Service Provider-Client Relationship in Context, *Journal of Marketing* 63(4) (October 1999), p. 38.

12. C. Noble and M. Mokwa, Implementing Marketing Strategies: Developing and Testing a Managerial Theory, *Journal of Marketing* 63(4) (October 1999), p. 57.

13. A. Weiss, E. Anderson, and D. MacInnis, Reputation Management As a Motivation for Sales Structure Decisions, *Journal of Marketing* 63(4) (October 1999), p. 74.

14. J. Graham, Customers for Keeps, *Selling Power* 16(3) (April 1996), pp. 50-51.

15. R. Jacob, Why Some Customers Are More Equal Than Others, *Fortune* (September 1994), pp. 215-224.

Chapter 3

1. K. Johnson, Mirror Your Prospects to Gain Their Trust, *Best's Review* (September 1994), pp. 76-81.

2. F. Gouillart and F. Sturdivant, Spend a Day in the Life of Your Customers, *Harvard Business Review* 72(1) (January/February 1994), p. 116.

3. L. Kellaway, Getting the Flavor of the Business, *Financial Times* (April 27, 1998), p. 11.

4. K. Blanchard, Get the Power, *Selling Power* (April 1998), p. 44.

5. T. Carter, *Contemporary Sales Force Management* (Binghamton, NY: The Haworth Press, 1998).

6. T. Kiely, Reengineering: It Doesn't Have to Be All or Nothing, *Harvard Business Review* 73(6) (November/December 1995), p. 16.

7. G. Brewer, Brain Power, *Sales and Marketing Management Magazine* (May 1997), p. 39.

8. J. Bessen, Riding the Marketing Information Wave, *Harvard Business Review* 71(5) (September/October 1993), p. 150.

9. R. Jacob, Beyond Quality and Value, *Fortune* (Autumn/Winter 1993), p. 8.

10. D. Dunn and C. Thomas, Reengineering Marketing, *Review of Business* (Spring 1996), p. 41.

11. J. Hyatt, Hot Commodity, Inc. (February 1996), p. 50.

12. M. Campanelli, Reshuffling the Deck, *Sales and Marketing Management Magazine* (June 1994), p. 83.

13. W. Keenan, Plugging into Your Customer's Needs, *Sales and Marketing Management Magazine* (January 1996), p. 62.

14. G. Brewer, Love the Ones You're With, *Sales and Marketing Management Magazine* (May 1996), p. 38.

15. R. Whiteley, Are You Driven to Action? *Sales and Marketing Management Magazine* (June 1994), p. 31.

16. R. Blattberg and J. Deighton, Manage Marketing by the Customer Equity Test, *Harvard Business Review* 76(1) (January/February 1998), p. 99.

17. K. Coyne and R. Dye, The Competitive Dynamics of Network Based Business, *Harvard Business Review* 76(1) (January/February 1998), p. 99.

18. T. Morrison, Meet the New Consumer, *Fortune* (Autumn/Winter 1993), p. 6.

19. E. Rasmusson, Winning Back Angry Customers, *Sales and Marketing Management Magazine* (October 1997), p. 131.

Chapter 4

1. R. Stillwell, Five Secrets to Keeping Your Clients, *LAN* (September 1994), p. 158.

2. T. Vavra, Selling After the Sale: The Advantages of Aftermarketing, *Supervision* (October 1994), pp. 9-11.

3. A. Zak, Recollection of Trusting and Nontrusting Behaviors in Intimate Relationships, *Psychological Reports* (June 1995), p. 1194.

4. B. Johanson and P. Nynes, Are Some Customers More Equal Than Others? *Harvard Business Review* 79(6) (November 2001), pp. 37-48.

5. T. Gruen, J. Summers, and F. Acito, Relationship Marketing Activities and Membership Behaviors in Professional Associations, *Journal of Marketing* 64(3) (July 2000), p. 34.

6. D. Stewart, Beginning Again: Change and Renewal in Intellectual Communities, *Journal of Marketing* 63(4) (October 1999), p. 2.

7. S. Rournier and D. Mick, Rediscovering Satisfaction, *Journal of Marketing* 63(4) (October 1999), p. 5.

8. D. Goleman, L. Price, and E. Arnold, Commercial Friendship: Service Provider-Client Relationship in Context, *Journal of Marketing* 63(4) (October 1999), p. 38.

9. M. Hartline, J. Maxham III, and D. McKee, Corridors of Influence in the Dissemination of Customer Oriented Strategy to Customer Contact Service Employees, *Journal of Marketing* 64(2) (April 2000), pp. 25-50.

10. D. Rya, Bank on Trust, *Selling Power* 19(2) (March 1999), p. 22.

11. J. Martin, Your Customers Are Telling the Truth, *Fortune* (February 16, 1998), pp. 161-168.

12. J. Cannon and C. Homburg, Buyer-Supplier Relationships and Customer Firm Cost, *Journal of Marketing* 65(1) (January 2001), p. 29.

13. R. Bagozzi and U. Dholakia, Goal Setting and Goal Striving in Consumer Behavior, *Journal of Marketing* 63 (Special Issue 1999), p. 19.

14. T. Carter, *Contemporary Sales Force Management* (Binghamton, NY: The Haworth Press, 1998), p. 12.

15. R. Achrol and P. Kotler, Marketing in a Network Economy, *Journal of Marketing* 63 (Special Issue 1999), p. 146.

16. Goleman, Price, and Arnold, Commercial Friendship, p. 38.

17. R. Srivastava, T. Shervani, and L. Fahey, Marketing Activities and the Discipline of Marketing, *Journal of Marketing* 63 (Special Issue 1999), p. 168.

18. C. Moorman and R. Rust, The Role of Marketing, *Journal of Marketing* 63 (Special Issue 1999), p. 180.

19. G. Williams and R. Miller, Change the Way You Persuade, *Harvard Business Review* 80(5) (May 2002), pp. 63-73.

20. T. Gruen, J. Summers, and F. Acito, Relationship Marketing Activities, Commitment and Membership Behaviors in Professional Associations, *Journal of Marketing* 64(3) (July 2000), p. 34.

21. D. Stewart, Beginning Again: Change and Renewal in Intellectual Communities, *Journal of Marketing* 63(4) (October 1999), p. 2.

22. J. Magretta, Why Business Models Matter, *Harvard Business Review* 80(5) (May 2002), pp. 86-92.

23. S. Fournier and D. Mick, Rediscovering Satisfaction, *Journal of Marketing* 63(4) (October 1999), p. 5.

24. Goleman, Price, and Arnold, Commercial Friendship, p. 38.

25. R. Oliver, Whence Customer Loyalty, *Journal of Marketing* 63 (Special Issue 1999), p. 33.

Chapter 5

1. D. Griffith and M. Harvey, An Intercultural Communication Model for Use in Global Markets, *Journal of International Marketing* 8(1) (2000), p. 6.

2. M. Fleschner, Signed, Sealed, Delivered, *Selling Power* 19(3) (April 1999), p. 42.

3. L. Comer and T. Drollinger, Active Empathic Listening and Selling Success: A Conceptual Framework, *Journal of Personal Selling and Sales Management* 19(1) (Winter 1999), p. 15.

4. R. Oliver, *Satisfaction* (Boston, MA: Irwin McGraw-Hill, 1997), pp. 17-68.

5. J. F. Sherry Jr., *Contemporary Marketing and Consumer Behavior* (Thousand Oaks, CA: Sage, 1995), pp. 1-34.

6. C. Christensen, The Innovator's Dilemma: When New Technologies Cause Great Firms to Fail (Boston, MA: Harvard Business School, 1997), pp. 29-61.

7. R. Sutton, The Weird Rules of Creativity, *Harvard Business Review* 79(8) (September 2001), p. 94.

8. P. Ghemawat, Distance Still Matters: The Hard Reality of Global Expansion, *Harvard Business Review* 79(8) (September 2001), p. 137.

9. L. Paulson, Customers for Life, *Executive Excellence* (September 1994), p. 12.

10. M. Prisbell, Strategies for Maintaining Relationships and Self-Related Competence in Ongoing Relationships, *Psychological Reports* (February 1995), p. 63.

11. T. Carter, Cultivation Council, *Selling Power* 19(3) (May 1999), pp. 100-102.

Chapter 6

1. M. Hartline, J. Maxham III, and D. McKee, Corridors of Influence in the Dissemination of Customer Oriented Strategy to Customer Contact Service Employees, *Journal of Marketing* 64(2) (April 2000), pp. 35-50.

2. J. Martin, Your Customers Are Telling the Truth, *Fortune* (February 16, 1998), pp. 161-168.

3. B. Johnson and P. Nunes, Are Some Customers More Equal Than Others? *Harvard Business Review* 79(10) (November 2001), pp. 37-48.

4. J. Weber, Management Lessons from the Best, *Business Week* (August 27, 2001).

5. G. Graham, If You Want Honesty, Break Some Rules, *Harvard Business Review* 80(4) (April 2002), p. 42.

6. P. Haspeslagh, T. Noda, and F. Boulos, Managing for Value: It's Not Just About the Numbers, *Harvard Business Review* 79(7) (July/August 2001), p. 64.

7. J. Green and G. Khermouch, Buzz Marketing, *Business Week* (July 30, 2001).

Chapter 7

1. P. Kotler, *Marketing Management* (New York: McGraw-Hill, 2000), p. 42.

2. D. Ray, Bank on Trust, *Selling Power* 19(2) (March 1999), p. 22.

3. Kotler, *Marketing Management*, p. 42; J. Cannon and C. Homburg, Buyer-Supplier Relationships and Customer Firm Cost, *Journal of Marketing* 65(1) (January 2001), p. 29.

4. P. Rogers, "Is Your Company Ready for One-to-One Marketing?" *Harvard Business Review* 77(1) (January/February 1999), pp. 151-160; R. Bagozzi and U. Dholakia, Goal Setting and Goal Striving in Consumer Behavior, *Journal of Marketing* 63 (Special Issue 1999), p. 19.

5. R. Oliver, Whence Customer Loyalty, *Journal of Marketing* 63 (Special Issue 1999), p. 33.

6. J. Bower and C. Gilbert, Disruptive Change, *Harvard Business Review* 80(5) (May 2002), pp. 95-101.

7. R. Achrol and P. Kotler, Marketing in a Network Economy, *Journal of Marketing* 63 (Special Issue 1999), p. 146.

8. R. Srivastava, T. Shervani, and L. Fahey, Marketing Activities and the Discipline of Marketing, *Journal of Marketing* 63 (Special Issue 1999), p. 168.

9. C. Moorman and R. Rust, The Role of Marketing, *Journal of Marketing* 63 (Special Issue 1999), p. 180.

10. T. Gruen, J. Summers, and F. Acito, Relationship Marketing Activities, Commitment, and Membership Behaviors in Professional Associations, *Journal of Marketing* 64(3) (July 2000), p. 34.

11. D. Stewart, Beginning Again: Change and Renewal in Intellectual Communities, *Journal of Marketing* 63(4) (October 1999), p. 2.

12. S. Fournier and D. Mick, Rediscovering Satisfaction, *Journal of Marketing* 63(4) (October 1999), p. 5.

13. Kotler, *Marketing Management*, p. 57.

14. D. Goleman, L. Price, and E. Arnold, Commercial Friendship: Service Provider-Client Relationship in Context, *Journal of Marketing* 63(4) (October 1999), p. 38.

15. C. Noble and M. Mokwa, Implementing Marketing Strategies: Developing and Testing a Managerial Theory, *Journal of Marketing* 63(4) (October 1999), p. 57.

16. A. Weiss, E. Anderson, and D. MacInnis, Reputation Management As a Motivation for Sales Structure Decisions, *Journal of Marketing* 63(4) (October 1999), p. 74.

17. T. Carter, *Contemporary Sales Force Management* (Binghamton, NY: The Haworth Press, 1998).

Chapter 8

1. J. Wolpert, Breaking Out of the Innovation Box, *Harvard Business Review* 80(8) (August 2002), pp. 77-83.

2. N. Bendapaudi and R. Leone, How to Lose Your Star Performer Without Losing Customers, Too, *Harvard Business Review* 79(10) (November 2001), pp. 104-112.

3. D. Rigby and C. Zook, Open Market Innovation, *Harvard Business Review* 80(10) (October 2002), pp. 80-89.

4. M. Merenda, Welcome Matters, *Bloomberg Wealth Manager* 15(2) (March 2003), pp. 21-23.

5. M. Pringle, Personal Interview, Lubrizol, Cleveland, Ohio, February 12, 2003.

6. B. Bathgate, Personal Interview, Lubrizol, Cleveland, Ohio, March 4, 2003.

7. R. Sethi, New Product Quality and Product Development Teams, *Journal of Marketing* 64(2) (April 2000), pp. 1-14.

8. E. Surratt, Personal Interview, Sony, London, England, March 14, 2003.

9. A. Latour, *The Wall Street Journal* (April 26, 2001), p. B6.

10. S. Kapner, Ericsson and Sony Discussing Mobile Phone Joint Venture, *The New York Times* (April 20, 2001), p. W1.

11. M. Musgrove, New Video-Game War: Microsoft, Nintendo Set to Offer Machines to Battle Sony PlayStation, *The Washington Post* (November 8, 2001), p. E1.

12. E. Harris, Ericsson Mix Technology Marketing Savvy—New Mobile-Phone Based Brand Aims to Topple Nokia: Just the Logo Is Ready, *The Wall Street Journal* (October 9, 2001), p. B9A.

13. M. Musgrove and A. Eunjung Cha, Xbox Enters the Fray: Microsoft Takes on Sony, Nintendo for the Share of $6.5 Billion Video-Game Market, *The Washington Post* (May 20, 2001), p. H1.

14. E. Surratt, Personal Interview, London, England, March 16, 2003.

Chapter 9

1. R. Armstrong and S. Min Yee, Do Chinese Trust Chinese? A Study of Chinese Buyers and Sellers in Malaysia, *Journal of International Marketing* 9(3) (2001), p. 63.

2. C. Craig and S. Douglas, Configural Advantage in Global Markets, *Journal of International Marketing* 8(1) (2000), p. 6.

3. K. Granzin and J. Painter, Motivation Influences on Buy Domestic Purchasing, *Journal of International Marketing* 9(2) (2000), pp. 73-96.

4. G. Knight, Entrepeneurship and Marketing Strategy, *Journal of International Marketing* 8(2) (2000), pp. 12-32.

5. W. Lazer and E. Shaw, Global Marketing Management: At the Dawn of the New Millennium, *Journal of International Marketing* 8(1) (2000), p. 65.

6. T. Carter, Cultivation Council, *Selling Power* 19(3), pp. 100-102.

7. T. Carter and M. Chattalas, Marketing Financial Services in London, *Services Marketing Quarterly* 22(4) (2001), pp. 63-81.

8. M. Hartline, J. Maxham III, and D. McKee, Corridors of Influence in the Dissemination of Customer Oriented Strategy to Customer Contact Service Employees, *Journal of Marketing* 64(2) (April 2000), pp. 35-50.

9. J. Martin, Your Customers Are Telling the Truth, *Fortune* (February 16, 1998), pp. 161-168.

10. B. Johnson and P. Nunes, Are Some Customers More Equal Than Others? *Harvard Business Review* 79(10) (November 2001), pp. 37-48.

11. J. Weber, Management Lessons from the Best, *Business Week* (August 27, 2001).

12. P. Engardio, Smart Globalization, *Business Week* (August 27, 2001), pp. 132-138.

13. A. Brady, Why Service Stinks, *Business Week* (October 23, 2000), pp. 118-128.

Index

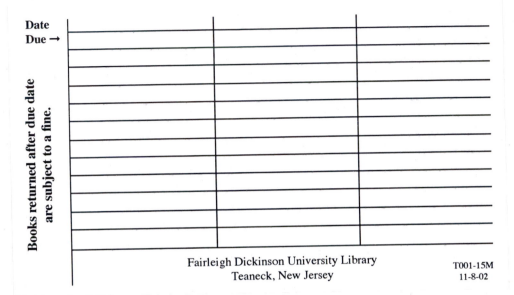

Date Due →

Books returned after due date are subject to a fine.